CHEAP TRICK

Books LLC®, Wiki Series, Memphis, USA, 2011. ISBN: 9781156419656. www.booksllc.net
Copyright: http://creativecommons.org/licenses/by-sa/3.0/deed.en

Table of Contents

Cheap Trick
Cheap Trick... 1
Cheap Trick discography 7

Cheap Trick albums
All Shook Up (Cheap Trick album).... 8
Busted (Cheap Trick album)............... 9
Cheap Trick (1977 album)................. 10
Cheap Trick (1997 album)................. 11
Dream Police.. 11
Found All the Parts 12
Heaven Tonight.................................. 13
In Color (album) 14
Lap of Luxury 15
Next Position Please 15
One on One (Cheap Trick album)..... 16

Rockford (album).............................. 17
Special One 17
Standing on the Edge (Cheap Trick album) 18
The Doctor (Cheap Trick album)...... 19
The Latest.. 19
Woke up with a Monster.................. 20

Cheap Trick members
Bun E. Carlos 20
Jon Brant 21
Randy Hogan 21
Rick Nielsen....................................... 22
Robin Zander..................................... 22
Tom Petersson................................... 23

Cheap Trick songs
Ain't That a Shame 23
California Man (song)....................... 24
Clock Strikes Ten 24
Day Tripper 25
Don't Be Cruel 26
Dream Police (song)......................... 26
Elo Kiddies... 27
I Want You to Want Me.................... 27
Mighty Wings 28
Need Your Love (song)..................... 28
Surrender (Cheap Trick song).......... 28
The Flame (Cheap Trick song) 29
Voices (Cheap Trick song)................ 29

Introduction

Purchase of this book entitles you to a free trial membership in the publisher's book club at www.booksllc.net. (Time limited offer.) Simply enter the barcode number from the back cover onto the membership form. The book club entitles you to select from hundreds of thousands of books at no additional charge. You can also download a digital copy of this and related books to read on the go. Simply enter the title or subject onto the search form to find them.

Each chapter in this book ends with a URL to a hyperlinked online version. Type the URL exactly as it appears. If you change the URL's capitalization it won't work. Use the online version to access related pages, websites, footnotes, tables, color photos, updates. Click the version history tab to see the chapter's contributors. Click the edit link to suggest changes.

A large and diverse editor base collaboratively wrote the book, not a single author. After a long process of discussion and debate, the chapters gradually took on a neutral point of view reached through consensus. Additional editors expanded and contributed to chapters striving to achieve balance and comprehensive coverage. This reduced the regional or cultural bias found in many other books and provided access and breadth on subject matter otherwise little documented.

Cheap Trick

Cheap Trick is an American rock band from Rockford, Illinois, formed in 1973. The band consists of members Robin Zander (lead vocals, rhythm guitar), Rick Nielsen (lead guitar, backing vocals), Tom Petersson (bass guitar, backing vocals), and Bun E. Carlos (drums, percussion).

Their biggest hits include "Surrender", "I Want You to Want Me", "The Flame",and "Dream Police"

As of 2009, Cheap Trick continues to tour with their most well known line-up. They have often been referred to in the Japanese press as the "American Beatles". In October 2007, the Illinois Senate passed a resolution designating April 1 as Cheap Trick Day in the state. The band was also ranked #25 in VH1's list of the *100 Greatest Artists of Hard Rock*.

History

Early years (1961–1974)

In 1961, Nielsen began playing locally in Rockford, Illinois utilizing an ever-increasing collection of rare and valuable guitars. He formed several local bands with names like The Boyz and The Grim Reapers. Brad Carlson later known as Bun E Carlos played in a rival Rockford band, the Pagans. Finally, Nielsen formed Fuse in 1967 with Tom

Peterson later known as Tom Petersson, who had played in yet another local band called The Bo Weevils.

Fuse released a self-titled album for Epic Records in 1970, which was generally ignored. Frustrated by their lack of success, Fuse recruited the two remaining members of Nazz in 1970 and ended up playing around the Midwest for 6–7 months under two monikers, Fuse or Nazz, depending on where they were gigging. With Bun E. Carlos joining on drums, Fuse moved to Philadelphia in 1971. They began calling themselves "Sick Man of Europe" in 1972–1973. After a European tour in 1973, Nielsen and Petersson returned to Rockford and reunited with Carlos.

Randy "Xeno" Hogan was the original lead singer for Cheap Trick. He left the band shortly after its formation and was replaced by Robin Zander.

Classic years (1975–1978)

Nielsen and Petersson performing in 1977

With Robin Zander now on vocals, the band recorded their first official demo in 1975 and played in warehouses, bowling alleys, and various other venues around the midwestern United States. The band was signed to Epic Records by A&R man Tom Werman, at the insistence of producer Jack Douglas who had seen the band perform in Wisconsin.

The band released their first album, *Cheap Trick*, in early 1977, which was produced by Jack Douglas. While favored by critics, the album was not successful in terms of sales. The album's lone single "Oh Candy" failed to chart. However, the band began to develop a fan base in Japan and "ELO Kiddies" was a hit single in Europe. Their second album *In Color* was released later that year and was produced by Tom Werman, who brought out their lighter and more pop-oriented side, producing an album much more polished than their first. However, the band bemoaned *In Color*'s production and would re-record it several years later. Moreover the album was largely unsuccessful. The singles "Southern Girls", "I Want You To Want Me", and "So Good To See You", failed to chart. However, "I Want You To Want Me" and "Clock Strikes Ten" were hit singles in Japan, with the latter going to #1 on the charts. *In Color* ultimately was ranked #448 on Rolling Stone magazine's list of the 500 greatest albums of all time.

The band's third album, *Heaven Tonight*, released in 1978 and again produced by Tom Werman, combined elements of the first two albums. Regarded by many fans and critics as their best album, the lead-off track "Surrender" was Cheap Trick's first single to chart in the United States, peaking at #62. It has gone on to become one of the band's signature songs. *Heaven Tonight* is also noteworthy as the first album recorded with a 12-string electric bass. Perhaps most importantly, this album made the band megastars in Japan.

Budokan brings success (1978–1981)

None of Cheap Trick's first three albums made it into the Top 40 in the United States. In Japan, however, all three albums became gold records. When Cheap Trick went to Japan to tour the country for the first time in April 1978, they were received with a frenzy reminiscent of Beatlemania. During this tour, Cheap Trick recorded two concerts attended by their loyal Japanese fans at the Nippon Budokan. Ten tracks taken from both shows were compiled and released as a live album titled *Cheap Trick at Budokan*, which was intended to be exclusive to Japan. Demand for the import album became so great that Epic Records finally released the album in the United States in 1979.

Cheap Trick performing in 1978 in Charlotte, NC, at the Park Center.

Cheap Trick at Budokan launched the band into international stardom, and the album went triple platinum in the United States. The smash track was the live version of "I Want You to Want Me," which had originally been released on *In Color*. It reached #7 on the Billboard Hot 100, and became Cheap Trick's biggest-selling single. The second single, "Ain't That A Shame," peaked at #35. One song from "At Budokan," "Need Your Love," had already been recorded for the next studio album that had already been finished but was temporarily shelved due to the unprecedented success of *At Budokan*. The album, titled *Dream Police* was released later in 1979 and was their third album in a row produced by Tom Werman. The title track of the album was a hit single, as was "Voices." Dream Police also found the band taking its style in a more experimental direction by incorporating strings and dabbling in heavy metal on tracks like "Gonna Raise Hell".

A four track EP entitled *Found All The Parts* was released in early 1980 and consisted of previously unreleased material. One side of the record contained live recordings and the other side had studio recordings. The live tracks were a faux live cover of The Beatles' "Day Tripper", and "Can't Hold On", a bluesy track performed at Budokan concerts 1978. The studio tracks were "Such A Good Girl" and "Take Me I'm Yours", which the record claims were recorded in 1975 and 1976, respectively. However, while they were older songs, they were recorded as a result of a session with Jack Douglas in early 1980. A total of nine tracks were recorded with Douglas, and remain obscure as they have only been issued on compilations, promotional samplers, and contest giveaways. For years, there was a false rumor that this was an album that had been rejected by Epic Records.

By mid-1980, when *All Shook Up* was released, Cheap Trick was headlining arenas. *All Shook Up*—produced by former Beatles producer George Martin—reached #24 on the charts and was certified gold, but the album's high-class background did not save it from descriptions like "Led Zeppelin gone psycho." Indeed, All Shook Up struck many fans of the band's earlier albums as too weird and experimental. One song from the *All Shook Up* sessions, "Everything Works If You Let It", appeared on the soundtrack of *Roadie*, and Nielsen and Carlos participated in sessions for John Lennon and Yoko Ono's album *Double Fantasy*.

Departure of Petersson (1981–1987)

On August 26, 1980, before the release of *All Shook Up*, Petersson left the group and went on to tour with various acts, eventually recording a solo album with his wife Dagmar, who had previously recorded with Kevin Coyne and others. The five-song mini-LP titled *Tom Petersson and Another Language* was released in 1984. Pete Comita replaced Petersson for the *All Shook Up* tour and the band recorded five songs with Comita to contribute to two movie soundtracks. "I'm The Man", "Born To Raise Hell", and "Ohm Sweet Ohm", which were produced by Jack Douglas, went to the film *Rock & Rule*. An accompanying soundtrack album for the film was never released and the songs weren't released until 1996 (on the *Sex, America, Cheap Trick* box set). "Reach Out" and "I Must Be Dreamin'" went to the film *Heavy Metal* and were produced by Roy Thomas Baker. "Reach Out" was written by Comita and Bob James. Comita left the band after completing the 1980-81 World Tour that promoted the "All Shook Up" album as well as the demo sessions for the band's forthcoming album. He would later claim that he co-wrote songs that appeared on the band's next two albums and was not credited. Jon Brant became Petersson's steady replacement. In July 1981, CBS Inc. sued Cheap Trick and their manager Ken Adamany for $10 million, alleging they were attempting to coerce CBS into re-negotiating their contract and had refused to record any new material for the label since October 1980. The lawsuit was settled in early 1982 and work commenced on the next album—*One on One*, produced by Roy Thomas Baker. The band changed direction again, this time opting for an album full of brash, shout-along hard rock songs. The album spawned two minor hits with the power ballad "If You Want My Love" and the innuendo-laced rocker "She's Tight." The music videos for both songs received heavy rotation on MTV.

The following year, Cheap Trick released *Next Position Please* with Todd Rundgren as producer. Rundgren downplayed the band's brash side and returned them to a more clean, pop-oriented sound similar to that of In Color. The album never found much of an audience and Cheap Trick's commercial fortunes were in decline. The first single was a cover of The Motors' "Dancing The Night Away." Epic Records, desperate for a hit from the band, forced the group to record the track, which had been a hit single in Europe. Rundgren refused to produce the song, and it was instead produced by *One On One* engineer Ian Taylor. It failed to chart, as did the second single and fan favorite "I Can't Take It". The Ian-Taylor-produced "Spring Break," which was a contribution to the soundtrack of the 1983 comedy film of the same name, was also issued as a single, which also failed to chart. In 1984, the band recorded the title track to the Tim Matheson comedy *Up The Creek*, which Nielsen later called "one of the worst" songs he'd ever written. The track reached #36 on Billboard's Top Tracks but was off the chart after two weeks.

In 1985 they were reunited with Jack Douglas, who had produced their debut album, to record *Standing on the Edge*. The band originally intended to return to their rough-sounding roots on the album, but Douglas backed out of the mixing process due to the legal issues he was having with Yoko Ono at the time. It was instead mixed by Tony Platt, who added more elements of typical 1980s production. This album was called their "best collection of bubblegum bazooka rock in years." The album also featured Mark Radice on keyboards, and he was also enlisted to assist in the songwriting process. The album's first single, "Tonight It's You", reached #8 on the Billboard's Top Rock Tracks chart and the video received heavy rotation on MTV. The following singles "Little Sister," and "How About You" failed to chart.

In 1986, the band recorded "Mighty Wings", the end-title cut for the film *Top Gun*. They then released *The Doctor*. Some of the songs contained elements of funk, and the band utilized female back-up vocalists for the first time. However, synthesizers and computer-programmed sound effects drowned out most of the prominent instruments, most noticeably the guitar. Produced by Tony Platt, it is widely considered the bands' worst album. The album's lone single, "It's Only Love" failed to chart, but many blame the album's poor success on the record label's lack of promotion. The music video for "It's Only Love" made history as the first music video to prominently use American Sign Language. *The Doctor* turned out to be the final album with Jon Brant as bassist, as Tom Petersson expressed interest in rejoining the band. Brant parted on good terms with the band, and has performed with the band a number of times since as a special guest or filling in for Petersson.

Lap of Luxury **(1987–1997)**

Petersson rejoined the group in 1987 and helped record 1988's *Lap of Luxury*, produced by Richie Zito. Due to the band's commercial decline, Epic Records forced the band to collaborate with professional songwriters. "The Flame", a typical '80s "factory ballad," was issued as the first single and became the band's first-ever #1 single. The second single, a cover of Elvis Presley's "Don't Be Cruel" also reached the top

10. Three other singles from the album were "Ghost Town", "Never Had A Lot To Lose", and "Let Go". Each one charted successfully, and *Lap of Luxury* went platinum and became recognized as the band's comeback album.

Busted was released in 1990 and was also produced by Richie Zito, as the band attempted to capitalize on the success of *Lap of Luxury*. This time, however, the band was allowed more creative control and professional songwriters were only used on a handful of songs. The first single "Can't Stop Falling Into Love" reached #12 on the charts but failed to reach as high as the label expected. The second single, the Diane Warren penned "Wherever Would I Be," suffered a worse fate reaching only #50. The following singles, "If You Need Me" and "Back N' Blue" were not successful, although the later single reached #32 on the US Mainstream Rock charts.

In 1991, Cheap Trick's *Greatest Hits* was released. It included twelve (twenty-eight on Japan pressing) of the band's most successful or popular singles and one new track, a cover of The Beatles' song "Magical Mystery Tour", which was an outtake from the *Lap Of Luxury* sessions.

In 1993, *Budokan II* was released. It featured the tracks that had been omitted from the original live album, plus three more tracks from their follow-up tour in 1979. The release was not authorized by the band, and it is now out of print. That same year, Robin Zander released his eponymous debut solo record on Interscope, produced by Jimmy Iovine. Guitarist Mike Campbell, best known for his work with Tom Petty and the Heartbreakers, collaborated with Zander on most of the album's tracks. The album was largely unsuccessful but the single "I've Always Got You" reached #13 on the US Mainstream Rock chart.

The group left Epic after the disappointing sales of "Busted" – to sign with Warner Bros. Records. In 1994 the band released *Woke Up With A Monster*, which was produced by producer Ted Templeman, best known for his work with Van Halen. The album's title track was issued as the first single and reached #16 on the US Mainstream Rock charts. The album's sales were poor, and it peaked at only #123. By the time the album came out, there had been a variety of significant changes in the band, both music-wise and appearance-wise. The style of music is more on the "hard rock" side, their "heaviest" album since *One On One*. Ted Templeman's heavy-handed production was also the subject of much criticism. Rick Nielsen grew a goatee, and Robin Zander's voice grew noticeably deeper. The band also contributed a cover of John Lennon's song "Cold Turkey" on the *Working Class Hero: A Tribute to John Lennon* album.

The band quickly parted ways with Warner Bros. and decided it was time to go back to the basics. They concentrated on the strength of their live shows, which were near-legendary, and they decided to release new recordings to independent labels instead of major companies. Over the next few years, Cheap Trick toured with several bands they had influenced, such as the Stone Temple Pilots and Pearl Jam. At the end of 1995, the band independently released *Gift*, a two track Christmas CD that benefited Chicago-area charities. They spent the next year recording demos with Tom Werman and Steve Albini. They then released the 7 inch vinyl single *Baby Talk/Brontosaurus* on Seattle-based indie label Sub Pop Records, which was produced by Albini. Now back on speaking terms with their former label, the band released Sex, America, Cheap Trick, a four disc box set that included dozens of rare and unreleased studio and live recordings along with some of the band's singles and favorites, on Epic Records. The collection, however, was criticized for lacking several of the band's most well-known and much-loved songs.

In 1997, Cheap Trick signed with indie label Red Ant Records and released *Cheap Trick*, produced by Ian Taylor, who the band had previously worked with in 1982 and 1983. The band attempted to re-introduce themselves to a new generation, as the album was self-titled and the artwork was similar to their first album which had been released twenty years before. Tom Werman would later claim that he had produced a track on the album and was not credited. The album was critically acclaimed and hailed as a return to form. Eleven weeks after the release, Red Ant's parent company Alliance Entertainment Corporation declared Chapter 11 bankruptcy. The single "Say Goodbye" only reached #119 on the charts, and the band again found themselves without a record label.

Cheap Trick Unlimited (1998–2005)

Cheap Trick began to rebuild in 1998 by trying to restore normal relations with Sony/Epic and the music retail community. They established their own record company, Cheap Trick Unlimited. They toured behind the release of *At Budokan: The Complete Concert*, and the remastered reissues of their first three albums. One of the multi-night stands from this tour resulted in Music for Hangovers, a vibrant live effort that featured members of The Smashing Pumpkins on two tracks.

Vocalist Robin Zander performing at Gulfstream Park in 2006.

Cheap Trick Unlimited sold the CD exclusively on Amazon.com for 8 weeks prior to releasing it in stores. To support the record they toured with Guided By Voices, and also played a concert with Pearl Jam. That same year, the band spent time in the studio recording with Steve Albini, who had produced the *Baby Talk/Brontosaurus* single. The band began re-recording their second album, *In Color*, as well as a handful of other miscellaneous tracks. The recordings were not finished and have yet to be officially released, but they were leaked onto the Internet. The band also revealed in an interview that a rarities album was in the works and initially planned for release in early 2000. However, it was never released.

In 1999, the band recorded a re-worked cover of Big Star's "In the Street" for use as the theme song for the television show *That '70s Show*. It was released on the show's soundtrack, *That '70s Album (Rockin')*. The group also re-recorded "Surrender," which was available exclusively at Getsigned.com.

In early 2000, Cheap Trick entered into a license with the now-defunct Musicmaker.com to directly download and create custom CDs for over 50 songs. After spending a good part of 2001 writing songs and about six weeks of pre-production, Cheap Trick went into Bearsville Studios in Woodstock, New York in March 2002, where the band put together their first studio album in six years, *Special One* in May 2003. At the same time, the band brought their record label to Big3 Entertainment. While the lead-off single "Scent of A Woman" was typical Cheap Trick fare, most of the album's tracks were acoustic-based. The album was met with mixed reviews, with one of the larger subjects of criticism being that the last two tracks on the album were basically the same song. The band also contributed the 1999 re-recorded version of "Surrender" to the comedy film Daddy Day Care and made a cameo in the film. They toured with Cake on the Unlimited Sunshine Tour that same year. In Japan, the band's entire catalog released between 1980 and 1990 was re-issued in remastered form.

In late 2003, Bun E. Carlos starred in a Target commercial with Torry Castellano, drummer of The Donnas.

In April, 2005, Cheap Trick released the five-track *Sessions@AOL* EP for digital download.

Independence (2006 onward)

In 2006, Cheap Trick released *Rockford* on Cheap Trick Unlimited/Big3 Records. The first single from the album was "Perfect Stranger" (produced by Linda Perry and co-written by Cheap Trick and Perry). The band promoted the album through appearances on the Sirius and XM satellite radio networks and a North American tour. That same year, "Surrender" was featured as a playable track in the hit video game Guitar Hero II, and the albums *Dream Police* and *All Shook Up* were re-issued in remastered form with bonus tracks. *One On One* and *Next Position Please (The Authorized Version)* were released as digital downloads. The band also appeared in a McDonald's advertising campaign called "This Is Your Wake-Up Call" featuring the band.

Guitarist Rick Nielsen performing at Gulfstream Park in 2006.

In 2007, officials of Rockford, Illinois honored Cheap Trick by reproducing the *Rockford* album cover art on that year's "city sticker" (vehicle registration). On June 19, 2007, the Illinois Senate passed Senate Resolution 255, which designated April 1 of every year as Cheap Trick Day in the State of Illinois. In August of that year, Cheap Trick honored the 40th anniversary of *Sgt. Pepper's Lonely Hearts Club Band* by playing the album in its entirety with the Hollywood Bowl Orchestra, conducted by Edwin Outwater, along with guest vocalists including Joan Osborne and Aimee Mann. Geoff Emerick, who engineered all the sound effects on *Sgt. Pepper*, engineered the same sounds for the two live concerts. The Chicago chapter of the National Academy of Recording Arts & Sciences honored Cheap Trick at the 2007 Recording Academy Honors event in Chicago on October 11, 2007. Nielsen and Carlos were on hand to receive the award, which was presented to them by Steve Albini.

In 2008, Cheap Trick were selected to be featured in the John Varvatos Spring/Summer 2008 clothing ad campaign. The black and white commercial put the group on a boardwalk with bicycles, the filming backdrop was a beach for a very modern look for the band. "California Man", a song written by Roy Wood and covered by the band on *Heaven Tonight* was used in the advertising promotion. On April 24, Cheap Trick played live at the Budokan for the 30th anniversary of the 1978 album *Live at Budokan*. On July 5, at their concert in Milwaukee, Rick Nielsen announced to the crowd that the show was being recorded for a future CD and/or DVD release. On November 11, the band released *At Budokan: 30th Anniversary Collectors Edition*, a box set that featured 3 CDs of the band's two concerts at Budokan recorded on April 28 and 30, 1978. A bonus DVD contained concert footage that originally aired on Japanese television, plus bonus features including footage from their return to Budokan for the original album's 30th anniversary.

Also in 2008, the song "Dream Police" was featured as a playable track in the hit video game Guitar Hero: Aerosmith. Rock Band 2 also featured the unreleased 1998 re-recorded version of "Hello There" as a playable track and it was also used for the game's opening sequence.

In an October, 2008 interview, Rick Nielsen revealed that several Cheap Trick releases were in store for the future, including a new album produced by Julian Raymond and Howard Willing, and the re-recorded version of *In Color*.

On April 4, 2009, it was announced the band would release a new album entitled *The Latest*. The album was released on June 23 only by preorder, and hit retail stores on July 21. It was also available in both vinyl and 8-track tape versions on the band's website. The group also performed the theme song for the film *Transformers: Revenge of the Fallen*. The group released *Sgt. Pepper Live*, their interpretation of the classic *Sgt. Pepper's Lonely Hearts Club Band* on August 25, 2009. This was released as both a compact disc and a DVD. 2009 also saw Bun E. Carlos launch a separate project including members of Smashing Pumpkins, Fountains of Wayne, and Hanson: *Tinted Windows*, a power pop quartet whose debut album quickly earned critical praise and repeat airplay on leading syndicated FM radio programs. The band headlined a homecoming show at the Allstate Arena in Rosemont, IL on Thursday, December 10, 2009 as the main act at the 104.3 WJMK-FM holiday show, Jack's Cheap Christmas.

In 2010, Cheap Trick's "Dream Police", re-recorded as "Green Police", appeared as the music bed in a controversial Audi commercial that first aired during the Super Bowl. The Audi commercial depicts a man enjoying his Audi TDI, which is apparently painlessly compliant with environmental regulations.

On March 19, 2010 it was announced that Bun E. Carlos was not currently the touring drummer for the band but remains a band member. Rick Nielsen's son Daxx is currently the touring drummer.

On April 6, 2010 Sony Music began to reissue Cheap Trick's albums that have been out of print via reissue specialist labels Friday Music and Wounded Bird Records. *One On One* and *Next Position Please* were released first and have been combined to fit on to one CD. *Standing On The Edge* and *The Doctor* were released separately and *Busted* was combined with the *Found All The Parts* EP.

On July 17, 2011 Cheap Trick were playing at Blues Fest in Ottawa, Ontario, Canada when a storm toppled the stage, destroying much electronic equipment. No one from the band was hurt in the incident. The band commented on their Facebook page, "Everyone is okay and we are so lucky to be alive and hope that all the fans are okay too,"

Legacy

Live performances

Cheap Trick is well known for their four decades of almost continuous touring. Their album Cheap Trick at Budokan (1978), along with Bob Dylan at Budokan (1979), elevated the status of the Budokan as a premier venue for rock concerts. On July 17, 2011, the stage that Cheap Trick were performing on at Ottawa, Canada's annual Bluesfest collapsed right on top of them due to high winds and a funnel cloud.

Instruments

Cheap Trick is known for its use - and large collection - of unusual and vintage guitars and basses.

Robin Zander has played a 1950s Rickenbacker Combo 450 Mapleglo since the late 1970s, as well as a Hamer 12-string guitar, a Gibson Firebird, and various Fender Telecaster-styled guitars.

Rick Nielsen is an avid collector who has over 250 guitars in his possession. He has collaborated with Hamer on trademark 'themed' guitars, some based on Cheap Trick albums such as "Rockford," "The Doctor," and even songs such as "Gonna Raise Hell." Hamer has also made unique five-necked guitars and electric mandocellos for Nielsen.

Tom Petersson is generally credited for having the initial idea for a 12-string bass. He previously had used an Alembic and Hagstrom 8-string basses, and asked Jol Dantzig of Hamer Guitars to make a 12-string bass. The company initially made him a 10-string bass. Following the successful trial use of that bass, the prototype 12-string bass, The Hamer 'Quad', was produced. Petersson later used 12-string basses made by Kids (a Japanese guitar maker), Chandler, and signature models from Waterstone. His primary choice of 4-string bass is a Gibson Thunderbird, though he also owns a very impressive array of 4, 5 and 8 stringed basses from other guitar makers. He is also an endorsee of Hofner basses.

Bun E. Carlos has played with many different commercial drum accessories, including Ludwig and Slingerland Radio King drums, Zildjian cymbals, rare Billy Gladstone snare drums, and Capella drum sticks. He is also an avid collector of vintage drums. Each year Carlos' collection can be seen at several drum shows in the Midwest.

Carlos has also recorded and written songs for many Rockford bands, such as Mark Willer and The Blues Hawks and also put together the short-lived Bun E. Carlos Experience, which also included Jon Brant, who replaced Tom Petersson in the mid '80s, on bass.

Band members

Current band members:
- Robin Zander – lead vocals, rhythm guitar, piano (1974–present)
- Rick Nielsen – lead guitar, backing vocals (1974–present)
- Tom Petersson – bass, backing vocals (1974–1980, 1987–present)
- Bun E. Carlos – drums, percussion (1974–present)

Former band members:
- Randy Hogan – lead vocals (1974)
- Pete Comita – bass, backing vocals (1980–1981)
- Jon Brant – bass, backing vocals (1981–1987, special guest and fill-in duties in 1999, 2004–05, & 2007)

Discography

Studio albums
- *Cheap Trick* (1977)
- *In Color* (1977)
- *Heaven Tonight* (1978)
- *Dream Police* (1979)
- *All Shook Up* (1980)
- *Found All The Parts* EP (2 live tracks, 2 studio tracks) (1980)
- *One on One* (1982)
- *Next Position Please* (1983)
- *Standing on the Edge* (1985)
- *The Doctor* (1986)
- *Lap of Luxury* (1988)
- *Busted* (1990)
- *Woke Up With A Monster* (1994)
- *Cheap Trick* (1997)
- *Special One* (2003)
- *Rockford* (2006)
- *The Latest* (2009)

Live albums
- *Cheap Trick at Budokan* (1978)
- *Found All The Parts* (1980)
- *Music for Hangovers* (1999)
- *Silver* (2001) Re-released (2004)
- *Sgt. Pepper Live* (2009)

Source (edited): "http://en.wikipedia.org/wiki/Cheap_Trick"

Cheap Trick discography

This page lists albums, singles, and compilations by the band **Cheap Trick**, alongside chart positions, release date (U.S.), and sales achievements (U.S.).

Live albums

- 1979: *Cheap Trick at Budokan*--(3x Multi-Platinum)
- 1993: *Budokan II*
- 1998: *Cheap Trick at Budokan: the Complete Concert*
- 1999: *Music for Hangovers*
- 2001: *Silver*
- 2005: *Sessions@AOL EP* (Digital download only)
- 2009: *Sgt. Pepper Live*

Compilations

- 1991: *The Greatest Hits*--(Platinum)(1x million)
- 1992: *Voices* (Int'l Marketing Grp)
- 1996: *Sex, America, Cheap Trick* (box set including unreleased tracks)
- 1996: *I Want You To Want Me* (IMG Records)
- 1998: *Hits of Cheap Trick* (Import) 16 Selected Hits
- 1998: *Don't Be Cruel* (Collectables Label) 9 Selected Singles
- 2000: *Authorized Greatest Hits*
- 2004: *The Essential Cheap Trick*
- 2005: *Collection (Cheap Trick/In Color/ Heaven Tonight)* Remastered and unreleased tracks from first 3 albums
- 2005: *Cheap Trick Rock On Break Out Years: 1979 (Madacy Records)*
- 2007: *Super Hits* (Sony Musical Specical Products)
- 2007: *Discover Cheap Trick* (Epic/Legacy Records)
- 2009: *Playlist: The Very Best of Cheap Trick* (Epic/Legacy Records)

Movie soundtracks

- 1979: *Over the Edge* "Surrender", "Speak Now or Forever Hold Your Peace", "Hello There", "Downed"
- 1980: *Roadie* "Everything Works If You Let It"
- 1981: *Heavy Metal* "Reach Out", "I Must Be Dreamin'"
- 1983: *Spring Break* "Spring Break"
- 1984: *Up the Creek* "Up the Creek"
- 1986: *Top Gun* "Mighty Wings"
- 1988: *Say Anything* "You Want It"
- 1988: *Caddyshack 2* "Money (That's What I Want)"
- 1990: *Queens Logic* "I Want You To Want Me"
- 1992: *Gladiator* "I Will Survive"
- 1992: *Encino Man* "Wild Thing"
- 1997: *Private Parts* "I Want You to Want Me"
- 1998: *Small Soldiers* "Surrender"
- 1999: *Detroit Rock City* "Surrender"
- 2001: *Joe Dirt* "If You Want My Love"
- 2003: *Daddy Day Care* "Surrender"
- 2009: *Transformers: Revenge of the Fallen* "Transformers (The Fallen Remix)"
- 2010: *Grown Ups (film)* "Just Got Back"

Singles

- From *Cheap Trick*:
  - 1977: "Oh Candy"
  - 1977: "ELO Kiddies"(Europe)
- From *In Color*
  - 1977: "I Want You To Want Me" - #1 JP, #97 Can
  - 1977: "Southern Girls"
  - 1977: "Clock Strikes Ten" (Japan) - #1 JP
  - 1978: "So Good To See You"
- From *Heaven Tonight*
  - 1978: "Surrender" - #62 US, #79 Can
  - 1978: "California Man"
- From *At Budokan*
  - 1979: "I Want You to Want Me" - #7 US, #29 UK, #2 Can, #15 Aus
  - 1979: "Ain't That a Shame" - #35 US, #10 Can
- From *Dream Police*
  - 1979: "Dream Police" - #26 US, #79 JP, #4 Can
  - 1979: "Voices" - #32 US, #12 Can, #16 Aus
  - 1980: "Way of the World" - #73 UK
  - 1980: "I'll Be With You Tonight"
- From *Roadie* (soundtrack)
  - 1980: "Everything Works If You Let It" - #44 US, #14 Can
- From *Found All The Parts*
  - 1980: "Day Tripper"
- From *All Shook Up*
  - 1980: "Stop This Game" - #48 US, #6 Can
  - 1980: "World's Greatest Lover"
- From *Heavy Metal* (soundtrack)
  - 1981: "Reach Out"
- From *One on One*
  - 1982: "If You Want My Love" - #45 US, #11 US Mainstream Rock, #57 UK, #2 Australia
  - 1982: "She's Tight" - #65 US
  - 1982: "Saturday at Midnight"
  - 1982: "I Want You" (Europe)
- From *Next Position Please*
  - 1983: "Dancing the Night Away"
  - 1983: "I Can't Take It"
  - 1983: "Next Position Please" (Europe)
- From *Spring Break* (soundtrack)
  - 1984: "Spring Break"
- From *Up the Creek* (soundtrack)
  - 1984: "Up the Creek" #36 US Mainstream Rock
- From *Standing on the Edge*
  - 1985: "Tonight It's You" - #44 US, #8 US Mainstream Rock
  - 1985: "Little Sister"
  - 1985: "How About You"
- From *Top Gun*
  - 1986: "Mighty Wings"
- From *The Doctor*
  - 1986: "It's Only Love"
  - 1986: "Kiss Me Red" (Europe)
- From *Lap of Luxury*
  - 1988: "The Flame - #1 US, #3 US Mainstream Rock, #77 UK. #1 Aus, #1 Can
  - 1988: "Don't Be Cruel" - #4 US, #8 US Mainstream Rock, #77 UK, #13 Aus
  - 1988: "Ghost Town" - #33 US, #32 US Mainstream Rock
  - 1989: "Never Had a Lot To Lose" - #75 US
  - 1989: "Let Go" - #35 US Mainstream Rock
- From *Busted*
  - 1990: "Can't Stop Fallin' Into Love" - #12 US, #4 US Mainstream Rock, #10 Can, #26 Aus-

tralia
- 1990: "Wherever Would I Be" - #50 US
- 1990: "If You Need Me"
- 1990: "Back N' Blue" - #32 US Mainstream Rock
- From *The Greatest Hits*
  - 1991: "Magical Mystery Tour"
- From *Woke Up With A Monster*
  - 1994: "Woke Up With A Monster" - #16 US Mainstream Rock
  - 1994: "You're All I Wanna Do"
  - 1994: "Girlfriends"
  - 1994: "Never Run Out of Love"
  - 1994: "Didn't Know I Had It"
- From *Working Class Hero: A Tribute to John Lennon*
  - 1995: "Cold Turkey"
- From *Cheap Trick*
  - 1997: "Say Goodbye" - #119 US, #39 US Mainstream Rock
  - 1997: "Baby No More"
  - 1997: "Baby Talk"
  - 1997: "Carnival Game"
- From *That '70s Show*
  - 1999: "That '70s Song"
- From *Special One*
  - 2003: "Scent of a Woman"
  - 2003: "My Obsession"
  - 2003: "Too Much"
- From *Rockford*
  - 2006: "Perfect Stranger"
  - 2006: "Come On, Come On, Come On"
  - 2006: "If It Takes a Lifetime"
- From *The Latest*
  - 2009: "Sick Man of Europe"

Video and DVD

- (2009) *Sgt. Pepper Live*
- (2008) *BUDOKAN!*
- (2004) *From Tokyo To You*
- (2002) *Music for Hangovers*
- (2001) *Silver*
- (1997) *Live from Australia*
- (1990) *Every Trick in the Book*

Source (edited): "http://en.wikipedia.org/wiki/Cheap_Trick_discography"

All Shook Up (Cheap Trick album)

All Shook Up is a 1980 album by Cheap Trick. It was their fifth studio album and sixth release overall. It was produced by former Beatles producer George Martin.

Overview

All Shook Up was even quirkier than its predecessor, the platinum-selling *Dream Police*. Many of its songs were less radio friendly and more experimental, and the cover art led many to question what the band was trying to accomplish. However, at the time, Cheap Trick had severed ties with long-time producer Tom Werman and took the opportunity to take their sound in a different direction. With the assistance of producer George Martin and engineer Geoff Emerick, many of the songs have a dimension not found on any other Cheap Trick album. "Stop This Game" was the only single to chart on the Billboard Hot 100, but "Just Got Back" and "World's Greatest Lover" continue to be fan favorites.

Track listing

All songs written Rick Nielsen, except where noted.

1. "Stop This Game" (Nielsen, Robin Zander) - 3:57
2. "Just Got Back" - 2:05
3. "Baby Loves to Rock" - 3:17
4. "Can't Stop It But I'm Gonna Try" - 3:31
5. "World's Greatest Lover" - 4:52
6. "High Priest of Rhythmic Noise" - 4:13
7. "Love Comes A-Tumblin' Down" - 3:08
8. "I Love You Honey But I Hate Your Friends" - 3:50
9. "Go For the Throat (Use Your Own Imagination)" - 3:04
10. "Who D'King" (Nielsen, Bun E. Carlos) - 2:18

Bonus tracks (2006 Reissue)

The bonus tracks on the reissue were all previously released. "Everything Works If You Let It" was on the soundtrack to *Roadie*, and the other four tracks were from the EP *Found All The Parts*.

11. "Everything Works If You Let It" (Nielsen) - 3:29
12. "Day Tripper" (live, short version) (Lennon/McCartney) - 3:41
13. "Can't Hold On" (live) - 5:55
14. "Such a Good Girl" - 3:04
15. "Take Me I'm Yours" - 4:34

Singles (Side A/Side B)

- "Everything Works If You Let It"/"Way of the World"/"Heaven Tonight" - #44 US, #14 Can
- "Stop This Game"/"Who D'King" - #48 US, #6 Can
- "World Greatest Lover"/"High Priest of Rhythmic Noise"

Outtakes

- "World's Greatest Lover" (Demo with Rick Nielsen on vocals, released on the *Sex, America, Cheap Trick* box set)
- "Machines Make Money" (Written and sung by Tom Petersson, unreleased)
- "Sleep Closes In" (Instrumental, unreleased)

Personnel

- Robin Zander - Lead Vocals, Rhythm Guitar
- Rick Nielsen - Lead Guitar, Backing Vocals, Art Direction, Design
- Tom Petersson - Bass, Backing Vocals
- Bun E. Carlos - Drums, Percussion

Additional personnel

- Geoff Emerick - Engineer
- Nigel Walker - Assistant Engineer
- Tony George - Assistant Engineer
- George Marino - Mastering
- Moshe Brakha - Photography
- George Martin - Arranger, Producer, Piano
- Ria Lewerke - Art Direction, Design

Background information

Right around the time of *All Shook Up*'s release, bassist Tom Petersson announced that he was leaving the band. He was replaced by Pete Comita.

The band performed the songs "Baby Loves to Rock" and "Can't Stop It But I'm Gonna Try" on the January 17, 1981 episode of *Saturday Night Live*.

There were several homages to The Beatles on this album. "Stop This Game" opens and closes with a droning piano note similar to the one that ends "A Day in the Life." The bridge to "Baby Loves to Rock" features the line "Not in Russia!" with the sound of an airplane in the background, a subtle reference to "Back in the U.S.S.R." "World's Greatest Lover" has vocals reminiscent of John Lennon.

"World's Greatest Lover" also cops the intro to "Big Balls"; Rick Nielsen wrote "Love Comes A-Tumblin' Down" for the recently deceased Bon Scott.

"Go For the Throat (Use Your Own Imagination) " references "(Get A) Grip (On Yourself)" by The Stranglers.

There were several outtakes from this outcome including: 01. Stop This Game 02. Stop This Game (Instrumental) 03. Can't Stop It But I'm Gonna Try 04. High Priest Of Rhythmic Noise 05. Love Comes A-Tumblin' Down 06. No Reason 07. Everything Works If You Let It (Acoustic Takes) 08. Everything Works If You Let It 09. Machines Make Money 10. Sleep Closes In 11. Merry Go Round 12. Why You're Here (Special One)

Trivia

"Just Got Back" is used in a montage in *Grown Ups* (film).

Singles - Billboard (North America) Source (edited): "http://en.wikipedia.org/wiki/All_Shook_Up_(Cheap_Trick_album)"

Busted (Cheap Trick album)

Busted is an album by Cheap Trick, which was released in 1990 and peaked at #44 on the US album charts. After the success of "The Flame" from the previous album Lap of Luxury, the band recorded *Busted* with a similar format, especially on the single "Can't Stop Fallin' Into Love." The single peaked at #12 on the US charts. The album failed to be as successful as the label had hoped, and about a year after the release of *Busted* Epic Records dropped Cheap Trick from their label. There were three videos shot for this LP; "Can't Stop Fallin' Into Love," "If You Need Me," and "Wherever Would I Be."

After being out of print for several years, the album was reissued in 2010 and combined onto one disc with the *Found All The Parts* EP from 1980, which made little sense since *Found All The Parts* was already available as bonus tracks on the 2006 reissue of the 1980 album *All Shook Up*. "Everything Works If You Let It", a track recorded for the soundtrack to the 1980 film *Roadie*, and the 1990 B-side "Big Bang" were also included on the disc.

The album was certified Gold in Canada for the sales of 50,000 copies in November 1990.

Track listing

1. "Back 'N Blue" (Johnson, Nielsen, Rhodes, Zander)
2. "I Can't Understand It" (R. Nielsen, R. Zander, T. Petersson)
3. "Wherever Would I Be" (D. Warren)
4. "If You Need Me" (M. Jones, R. Nielsen, R. Zander)
5. "Can't Stop Fallin' Into Love" (R. Nielsen, R. Zander, T. Petersson, L. Nesbit)
6. "Busted" (R. Nielsen, R. Zander)
7. "Walk Away" (R. Nielsen, R. Zander, T. Petersson, C. Hynde)
8. "You Drive, I'll Steer" (R. Nielsen, R. Zander)
9. "When You Need Someone" (N. Graham, Kelly, R. Nielsen)
10. "Had To Make You Mine" (R. Nielsen, R. Zander, T. Petersson)
11. "Rock 'N' Roll Tonight" (R. Wood)

Japanese Version

12. "Big Bang" (R. Nielsen, R. Zander)

2010 Reissue (Combined with the *Found All The Parts* EP)

1. "Day Tripper" [Live] (J. Lennon, P. McCartney)
2. "Can't Hold On" [Live] (R. Nielsen)
3. "Such a Good Girl" (R. Nielsen)
4. "Take Me I'm Yours" (R. Nielsen)
5. "Back 'N Blue" (Johnson, Nielsen, Rhodes, Zander)
6. "I Can't Understand It" (R. Nielsen, R. Zander, T. Petersson)
7. "Wherever Would I Be" (D. Warren)
8. "If You Need Me" (M. Jones, R. Nielsen, R. Zander)
9. "Can't Stop Fallin' Into Love" (R. Nielsen, R. Zander, T. Petersson, L. Nesbit)
10. "Busted" (R. Nielsen, R. Zander)
11. "Walk Away" (R. Nielsen, R. Zander, T. Petersson, C. Hynde)
12. "You Drive, I'll Steer" (R. Nielsen, R. Zander)
13. "When You Need Someone" (N. Graham, Kelly, R. Nielsen)
14. "Had To Make You Mine" (R. Nielsen, R. Zander, T. Petersson)
15. "Rock 'N' Roll Tonight" (R. Wood)
16. "Everything Works If You Let It" (R. Nielsen)
17. "Big Bang" (R. Nielsen)

Singles

- (1990) "Can't Stop Fallin' Into Love/You Drive, I'll Steer" - #12 US, #4 US Mainstream Rock, #10 Can, #26 Australia
- (1990) "Wherever Would I Be/Busted" - #50 US
- (1990) "If You Need Me/Big Bang"
- (1990) "Back N' Blue" - #32 US Mainstream Rock

Background Information

Chrissie Hynde of The Pretenders recorded guest vocals on "Walk Away."

The demo version of "Can't Stop Fallin' Into Love" featured blues singer/songwriter Harvey Scales on vocals.

"If You Need Me" was a re-written version of a song titled "Don't Ever Let Me Go," an outtake from 1985's *Standing On The Edge* album.

"Rock 'N' Roll Tonight" was a song

that the band had been performing live since their early days.

Source (edited): "http://en.wikipedia.org/wiki/Busted_(Cheap_Trick_album)"

Cheap Trick (1977 album)

Cheap Trick is a studio album released in 1977 by the American rock band Cheap Trick. It was their debut album, produced by Jack Douglas.

Overview

Most of the songs have a more raw sound akin to hard rock bands of the period compared to the group's later more polished power pop style, and the song lyrics deal with more extreme subject matter than later albums. For instance, "The Ballad of T.V. Violence" is about serial killer Richard Speck, "Daddy Should Have Stayed in High School" is about a pedophile, and "Oh Candy" is about a friend of the band who committed suicide.

This album, along with the following three albums, are considered by fans and critics to be Cheap Trick's best works. This one, however, is more known for capturing both their dark side and the fierceness of their early live performances more than any other studio release in their catalog.

The album was produced by Jack Douglas, who had achieved a similar sonic density with the blues-rock/hard rock Aerosmith, and the album sounds quite different than subsequent Cheap Trick records. Jack Douglas later worked with the band on the Found All The Parts EP, the album *Standing On The Edge*, as well as a re-recorded version of "Surrender" in the late 1990s and a few tracks on *Rockford*.

Track listing

All songs written by Rick Nielsen except where noted.

Side A

1. "Hot Love" — 2:30
2. "Speak Now or Forever Hold Your Peace" (Terry Reid) — 4:35
3. "He's a Whore" — 2:43
4. "Mandocello" — 4:47
5. "The Ballad of T.V. Violence (I'm Not the Only Boy)" — 5:15

Side 1

1. "ELO Kiddies" — 3:41
2. "Daddy Should Have Stayed in High School" — 4:44
3. "Taxman, Mr. Thief" — 4:16
4. "Cry, Cry" (Nielsen, Robin Zander, Tom Petersson) — 4:22
5. "Oh, Candy" — 3:07

Bonus tracks (1998 Reissue)

The 1998 reissue of *Cheap Trick* was released with five bonus tracks, including an early studio version of their later hit "I Want You To Want Me."

11. "Lovin' Money" — 4:09
12. "I Want You To Want Me" — 2:43
13. "Lookout" — 3:30
14. "You're All Talk" (Nielsen, Petersson) — 3:31
15. "I Dig Go-Go Girls" — 3:06

Singles

- 1977: "Oh Candy b/w Daddy Should Have Stayed in High School"
- 1977: "ELO Kiddies b/w Speak Now Or Forever Hold Your Peace" (Europe)

Unreleased Outtakes

- "Disco Paradise"
- "Surrender" (Later re-recorded for their third album *Heaven Tonight*)
- "Auf Wiedersehen" (Also later re-recorded for their third album *Heaven Tonight*)
- "Ultramental" (Later reworked and became the title track to the album *Dream Police*)

Personnel

- Robin Zander – lead vocals, rhythm guitar
- Rick Nielsen – lead guitar, vocals
- Tom Petersson – bass guitar, vocals
- Bun E. Carlos – drums

Additional personnel

- Jack Douglas - producer
- Jay Messina - engineer
- Sam Ginsberg - assistant engineer

Background information

The original vinyl record had "Side A" printed on one side of the label and "Side 1" printed on the other, a humorous touch reflecting the band's conviction that they didn't have any "B" material, although the placement of the track listing on the jacket seemed to indicate "Hot Love" was the first track on the album. Indeed, the matrix numbers on the record show the "Hot Love" side was designated side A and the "Elo Kiddies" side as side B. When the album was released on compact disc in the mid-1980s, it followed the same sequence. However, when the album was reissued on CD in 1998, the band's preferred sequence was used, with "Elo Kiddies" being the first track.

When Cheap Trick performed the entire debut album at the Metro Club in Chicago on May 1, 1998, they played the album in the intended order, starting with "Elo Kiddies". This concert was recorded, and parts of it contributed to the live album *Music for Hangovers*.

When Rick Nielsen was working with John Lennon on *Double Fantasy* he told him about when the band was preparing to record their debut album they were trying to decide on a producer. Figuring they had nothing to lose, they sent a letter to Lennon requesting him but never got a reply. Lennon said he never received the letter but would loved to have done it.

Other

Big Black released a cover of "He's a Whore" as a single. The single cover was a remake in the style of the original album cover. The song was later included on the CD release of Big Black's second album, *Songs About Fucking*.

In the documentary End of the Century: The Story of the Ramones, Johnny Ramone states that the guitar riff of

"The KKK Took My Baby Away" was inspired by the riff of "He's a Whore"

The Methadones cover "He's a Whore" on 21st Century Power Pop Riot. A cover record released in 2006.

Sugar High recorded a version of "Oh Candy" on their 2008 release "Let the Sunshine Out".

Source (edited): "http://en.wikipedia.org/wiki/Cheap_Trick_(1977_album)"

Cheap Trick (1997 album)

Cheap Trick, commonly referred to as **Cheap Trick '97**, is an eponymous album by the American rock band Cheap Trick, produced by the band and Ian Taylor and released on Red Ant Records and Alliance Entertainment. The album is referred to as "Cheap Trick II" when it is referenced on the promotional DVD that was released with the band's *Special One* album in 2003. Ian Taylor had previously engineered the *One On One* LP in 1982 and produced a handful of other tracks in 1983 including the single "Dancin' The Night Away" for the *Next Position Please* LP as well as the contributions that the band recorded for the 1983 Sean S. Cunningham comedy film *Spring Break*.

Named after their original 1977 eponymous debut, the album features a similar black-and-white scheme on the cover and a similar stripped-down sound to what they had used 20 years earlier. (In a twist of irony, Rick Nielsen and Bun E. Carlos are represented on the front cover (rather than the back) of a Cheap Trick album for the first and only time, likewise Robin Zander and Tom Petersson are relegated to the back, but their gear appears instead of the band members themselves.) Some have suggested that the band chose this approach treating their debut with Red Ant/Alliance as an opportunity to re-introduce themselves as a band to a new era. Red Ant filed for bankruptcy three weeks after the album's release. There was one black-and-white video shot for the LP; "Say Goodbye." The Japanese version of the album featured a different album cover, a black-and-white photo of the band members.

The album is now only available as a digital download at various online retailers, although a limited edition reissue was released in Japan in 2004.

Track listing

All tracks by Rick Nielsen, Tom Petersson & Robin Zander except where noted

1. "Anytime" – 4:36
2. "Hard to Tell" – 4:07
3. "Carnival Game" (Jerry Dale McFadden, Nielsen, Petersson, Robert Reynolds, Zander) – 3:50
4. "Shelter" (Jamie Mica, Nielsen, Petersson, Zander) – 4:13
5. "You Let a Lotta People Down" – 4:29
6. "Baby No More" – 2:54
7. "Yeah Yeah" – 3:12
8. "Say Goodbye" – 3:34
9. "Wrong All Along" – 2:18
10. "Eight Miles Low" – 3:28
11. "It All Comes Back to You" (Jerry Dale McFadden, Nielsen, Petersson, Robert Reynolds, Zander) – 3:41

Bonus Tracks

This album came with a hidden "track 0" which is a 2:58 montage of clips of songs on the album and studio banter. Some copies of this album came with a bonus disc that contained two songs that were produced by Steve Albini. "Baby Talk" was written by Rick Nielsen, Robin Zander, and Tom Petersson. "Brontosaurus" is a 1970 Roy Wood composition, originally recorded by The Move. The tracks were originally released on 7 inch vinyl by Sub Pop Records in 1996. They are also bonus tracks on the Japanese and digital download versions of the album.

1. "Baby Talk"
2. "Brontosaurus"

Singles

- (1997) "Say Goodbye/Yeah Yeah" - #119 US, #39 US Mainstream Rock
- (1997) "Baby No More/Anytime/Brontosaurus"
- (1997) "Carnival Game/You Let a Lotta People Down"

Personnel

- Mike Beert – Cello
- Richie Cannata – Piano
- Bun E. Carlos – Cymbals, Drums, Tambourine
- Rick Nielsen – Acoustic & Electric Guitar, Piano, Vocals, Speech/Speaker/Speaking Part, Ebo, Electric Saw
- Tom Petersson – Acoustic Guitar, Bass, Vocals, Tamboura, Bass Viol, Ebo, Acoustic Bass, 12-String Bass Guitar
- Ian Taylor – Producer, Engineer, Mixing
- Robin Zander – Acoustic & 12 Sting Guitar, Piano, Vocals, Slide Guitar, Tiple

Source (edited): "http://en.wikipedia.org/wiki/Cheap_Trick_(1997_album)"

Dream Police

Dream Police is a 1979 studio album by Cheap Trick. It was their fourth studio release, and third in a row produced by Tom Werman. It is the band's most commercially successful studio album, going to #6 on the Billboard 200 and being certified platinum within a few months of its release.

Overview

Dream Police shows the band expanding into longer, more complex songs and incorporating orchestration on several tracks. Three videos were produced: "Dream Police", "Way of The World" and "Voices".

The album's title track became a Top 30 hit for the band. "Voices" was also a hit for the band, reaching #32 on the Billboard chart.

"Voices" has been used twice on *How I Met Your Mother*.

Near the end of "Gonna Raise Hell" the orchestra are citing a snippet from "Heaven Tonight".

Variations

In 2010, Cheap Trick re-recorded the title track as **Green Police** for the controversial Green Police advertisement which aired during Super Bowl XLIV for Audi.

Track listing

1. "Dream Police" (Rick Nielsen) – 3:49
2. "Way of the World" (Robin Zander, Nielsen) – 3:39
3. "The House Is Rockin' (With Domestic Problems)" (Tom Petersson, Nielsen) – 5:12
4. "Gonna Raise Hell" (Nielsen) – 9:20
5. "I'll Be with You Tonight" (Nielsen, Bun E. Carlos, Petersson, Zander) – 3:52
6. "Voices" (Nielsen) – 4:22
7. "Writing on the Wall" (Nielsen) – 3:26
8. "I Know What I Want" (Nielsen) – 4:29
9. "Need Your Love" (Nielsen, Petersson) – 7:39

Bonus tracks (2006 Reissue)

The 2006 reissue of *Dream Police* consisted mainly of rare live versions of songs from the album. "I Know What I Want" is noteworthy for being the b-side to their 1988 single "Don't Be Cruel," and the only non-live track is a demo of the title track without its trademark strings.

10. "The House Is Rockin' (With Domestic Problems)" (live) - 6:16
11. "Way of the World" (live) - 3:59
12. "Dream Police" (No Strings Version) - 3:52
13. "I Know What I Want" (live) - 4:43

Singles

- 1979: "Dream Police" b/w "Heaven Tonight" – #26 US, #4 Canada, #79 Japan
- 1979: "Voices" b/w "Surrender" (Live) – #16 Australia (UK)
- 1979: "Voices" b/w "The House Is Rockin' (With Domestic Problems)" – #32 US, #12 Canada,(US & Canada)
- 1980: "Way Of The World" b/w "Oh Candy" – #73 UK
- 1980: "I'll Be With You Tonight" b/w "He's A Whore" & "So Good To See You" (UK)

Unreleased Outtakes

- "Next Position Please" (Later re-recorded in 1983 as the title track for the album of the same name)
- "It Must Be Love" (This song was given to Rick Derringer who covered it on his 1979 album *Guitars and Women*)
- "See Me Now" ("Way of the World" with alternate lyrics)
- "Voices" (With Tom Petersson on vocals)
- "I Know What I Want" (With Robin Zander on vocals)

Singles - Billboard

Personnel

- Robin Zander – lead vocals, rhythm guitar
- Rick Nielsen – lead guitar, background vocals
- Tom Petersson - bass guitar, background vocals, lead vocals on "I Know What I Want"
- Bun E. Carlos – drums, percussion

Additional personnel

- Ken Adamany - Assistant
- Mike Beiriger - Engineer
- Steve Dessau - Design
- Gary Ladinsky - Engineer
- Steve Lukather - Guitar on "Voices"
- George Marino - Mastering
- Reid Miles - Photography
- Paula Scher - Design
- Tom Werman - Producer
- Jai Winding - Organ, Piano, Keyboards

Source (edited): "http://en.wikipedia.org/wiki/Dream_Police"

Found All the Parts

Found All the Parts is an EP released by Cheap Trick in 1980. It was released on a 10" disc as part of Epic Records' short-lived Nu-Disk series. The EP also contained a bonus promotional 7" single of "Everything Works If You Let It". *Found All the Parts* was reissued in 12" format in 1983.

"Day Tripper" was not actually recorded live. While the band had recorded a live cover of the song, they did not like the way it had turned out. It was re-recorded in the studio with the live crowd from the original track added in. "Can't Hold On" was from the famed *At Budokan* concert in 1978 and has since been included on the *Budokan II* and *At Budokan: The Complete Concert* albums. "Such A Good Girl" and "Take Me I'm Yours" were recorded with producer Jack Douglas between December 1979 and January 1980, not 1976 and 1977 as the album claims. Several other tracks were recorded during the same sessions, most of which are scarce or still remain unreleased (see outtakes below).

This EP is currently available as bonus tracks to the 2006 remastered reissue of the *All Shook Up* album in every region except Japan, were it was reissued in remastered form on its own in 2003.

Track listing

Side 1

1. "Day Tripper" (Live) (John Lennon, Paul McCartney) – 3:17
2. "Can't Hold On" (Live) (Rick Nielsen) – 5:56

Side 2
1. "Such a Good Girl" (Nielsen) – 3:00
2. "Take Me I'm Yours" (Nielsen, Robin Zander) – 4:31

Outtakes
- "I Need Love" (Available on the *Sex, America, Cheap Trick* box set)
- "Loser" (Available on the *Legacy Rock Experience* sampler)
- "Oh Boy (w/Vocals)" (Available on the *Oh Boy (Demo)/If You Want My Love (Demo)* promotional single)
- "Fan Club" (Available on a "Trickfest (I)" prize cassette)
- "Ain't Got You" (Available on the "Trickfest (I)" prize cassette)
- "You Talk Too Much" (Available on the "Trickfest (I)" prize cassette, later re-recorded for the album *Next Position Please*)
- "I Was A Fool" (Unreleased)

Personnel
- Robin Zander – lead vocals, rhythm guitar
- Rick Nielsen – lead guitar, vocals
- Tom Petersson – bass guitar, vocals
- Bun E. Carlos – drums

Source (edited): "http://en.wikipedia.org/wiki/Found_All_the_Parts"

Heaven Tonight

Heaven Tonight is Cheap Trick's third album, released in 1978. The album was remastered and released with bonus tracks on Sony's Epic/Legacy imprint in 1998. The album cover features lead singer Robin Zander and bassist Tom Petersson.

Heaven Tonight is considered Cheap Trick's best album by many fans and critics. While their debut album *Cheap Trick* showed the band's darker, rawer side and *In Color* showed their lighter, poppier side, *Heaven Tonight* combined both elements to produce a hook-filled pop-rock album with an attitude. Popular songs from this album include the anthemic "Surrender", "Auf Wiedersehen", the title track, and a cover of The Move's "California Man".

Heaven Tonight is also known as the first album ever recorded with a 12-string electric bass.

Overview

This was the second Cheap Trick album to feature Robin Zander and Tom Petersson on the front cover and Bun E. Carlos and Rick Nielsen on the back. While the front cover has Zander and Petersson standing in front of a nondescript background, the back cover portion (part of a continuous, wrap-around shot on the original LP) reveals that they are standing inside a public restroom where Nielsen is brushing his teeth and Carlos is fixing his tie in the mirror. Nielsen has a cassette copy of the band's previous album, *In Color* sticking out of his back pocket. At the suggestion of the record company, the album was originally to be called *American Standard*; the cover photography was intended to play upon the secondary association with the well-known manufacturer of plumbing fixtures. The band were less pleased with the idea and opted for the release title, but the cover design remained.

"Surrender" was the only song from this album released on the original version of the 1979 live album *Cheap Trick at Budokan*. On the 1998 reissue *At Budokan: The Complete Concert*, three additional songs from this album were included - "Auf Wiedersehen", "High Roller" and "California Man".

"Oh Claire" is a one-minute live jam with "Oh, Konnichiwa" as the only lyrics. The title is a pun on Eau Claire, Wisconsin, where the band used to play frequently in their pre-stardom days. Cheap Trick wrote a similarly titled song, "O Claire," for their 2006 album *Rockford*. "How Are You" contains, in its second verse, the extract of "The Lord's Prayer", sped up 10 times.

"Surrender" is featured as a playable song on the video game *Guitar Hero II*.

Track listing

All songs written by Rick Nielsen, except where noted.

Side One
1. "Surrender" – 4:16
2. "On Top of the World" – 4:01
3. "California Man" (Roy Wood) – 3:44
4. "High Roller" (Rick Nielsen, Tom Petersson, Robin Zander) – 3:58
5. "Auf Wiedersehen" (Nielsen, Petersson) – 3:42

Side Two
1. "Takin' Me Back" – 4:52
2. "On the Radio" – 4:33
3. "Heaven Tonight" (Nielsen, Petersson) – 5:25
4. "Stiff Competition" – 3:40
5. "How Are You?" (Nielsen, Petersson) – 4:21
6. "Oh Claire" (Bun E. Carlos, Nielsen, Petersson, Zander) – 1:10 (not listed on LP label or album cover)

Bonus tracks (1998 Reissue)
12. "Stiff Competition" (Outtake) – 4:03
13. "Surrender" (Outtake) – 4:52

Singles (Side A/Side B)
- (1978) "Surrender/Auf Wiedersehen" - #62 US
- (1978) "California Man/Stiff Competition"
- (1978) "California Man/I Want You To Want Me (Live version from AT BUDOKAN)"

Personnel
- Robin Zander – lead vocals, rhythm guitar
- Rick Nielsen – lead guitar, backing vocals
- Tom Petersson – bass, backing vocals
- Bun E. Carlos – drums

Additional personnel
- Jai Winding – keyboards
- Paula Scher – design

Source (edited): "http://en.wikipedia.

In Color (album)

In Color is the second studio album by Cheap Trick, released in 1977. It was produced by Tom Werman.

This album is considered a classic of the power pop genre as well as one of the best rock albums ever recorded. The album was ranked #4 at Shake Some Action: The Ultimate Power Pop Guide. In 2003, the album was ranked number 448 on *Rolling Stone* magazine's list of the 500 greatest albums of all time.

Overview

In Color, as opposed to the band's self-titled debut, features a more polished production in the hopes of making a commercial impact. While the band members complained that the album lost its power through Tom Werman's overproduction, *In Color* does show the band's more melodic side that was partially lost on the debut.

The album made the band superstars in Japan, where "I Want You to Want Me" and "Clock Strikes Ten" were hit singles, with the latter hitting #1 on the Japanese charts.

Re-recorded version

In Color was re-recorded by the band in 1998 with producer Steve Albini. The band's intention was to record the album on their own terms and for the songs to sound the way that they had originally intended. However, the album was never officially completed or released, but it was leaked onto the internet along with a handful of other tracks recorded during the same session.

In September 2008, the re-recorded version of "Hello There" was featured in the trailer of upcoming video game *Rock Band 2*, raising suspicions that the album may have been finished, or at least that track. "Hello There" had been previously announced as a playable track, but it was unknown which version. "Oh Boy," the B-side to the single for "I Want You To Want Me" was re-recorded with vocals in 1980. It was released in 2003 on the "Oh Boy (Demo)/If You Want My Love (Demo)" promotional seven-inch vinyl record.

In April 2010, Rick Nielsen confirmed to the online music site Spinner that the band had in fact finished re-recording the album and planned to release the new version in "the not so distant future"

Track listing

All songs written by Rick Nielsen, except where noted.

Side One
1. "Hello There" – 1:41
2. "Big Eyes" – 3:10
3. "Downed" – 4:12
4. "I Want You to Want Me" – 3:11
5. "You're All Talk" (Rick Nielsen, Tom Petersson) – 3:36

Side Two
1. "Oh Caroline" – 2:59
2. "Clock Strikes Ten" – 2:59
3. "Southern Girls" (Nielsen, Petersson) – 3:44
4. "Come On, Come On" – 2:41
5. "So Good to See You" – 3:37

Bonus tracks (1998 Reissue)

The 1998 reissue of *In Color* featured five bonus tracks, including "Oh Boy," which was the b-side to "I Want You to Want Me," and "Goodnight," the live show-closing variation on "Hello There."

11. "Oh Boy" (Instrumental version) – 3:09
12. "Southern Girls" (Demo) (Rick Nielsen, Tom Petersson) – 3:03
13. "Come On, Come On" (Demo) – 2:04
14. "You're All Talk" (Live) (Rick Nielsen, Tom Petersson) – 3:41
15. "Goodnight" (Live) – 2:19

Unreleased Outtakes
- "Please Mrs. Henry" (Instrumental, Bob Dylan cover)

Singles (Side A/Side B)
- 1977: "I Want You To Want Me/Oh Boy"
- 1977: "Southern Girls/You're All Talk"
- 1977: "Clock Strikes Ten/So Good To See You" (Japan) #1 JAP
- 1978: "So Good To See You/You're All Talk"

Personnel
- Robin Zander - lead vocals, rhythm guitar
- Rick Nielsen - lead guitars, vocals
- Tom Petersson - bass, vocals
- Bun E. Carlos - drums

Additional personnel
- Tom Werman - producer
- Antonino Reale - engineer
- George Marino - mastering

Background information

Five of the ten tracks on *In Color* were later released in live form on Cheap Trick's classic live album *At Budokan* ("Hello There," "Big Eyes," "I Want You to Want Me," "Clock Strikes Ten" and "Come On, Come On").

In Color's front cover has a color photo of Zander and Petersson sitting on motorcycles with the words "Cheap Trick, In Color." across the top. Its back cover has an upside-down black-and-white photo of Carlos and Nielsen sitting on bicycles with the words "And In Black and White." across the top.
Source (edited): "http://en.wikipedia.org/wiki/In_Color_(album)"

Lap of Luxury

Lap of Luxury is the tenth studio album by Cheap Trick. Released in 1988, it is the band's second most commercially successful studio album, going to #16 on the Billboard 200 (trailing only 1979's *Dream Police* which went to #6) and has been certified platinum in sales.

The album was certified Platinum in Canada for the 100,000 sales in September 1988.

Overview

Although considered a comeback album for Cheap Trick, it was actually another record created in the midst of much turmoil with their label at the time, Epic Records. Before its recording, original bassist Tom Petersson rejoined the group and Epic had determined that it was going to help with some of the songwriting, and the band acquiesced only to save their contract. Ironically, the Mainstream Ballad The Flame became a #1 hit single, and the album went platinum. However, the band still points to this album as the one that restricted their range and boxed them into a sound that would eventually stall their recording career for most of the 1990s.

Track listing

1. "Let Go" (R. Nielsen, Todd Cerney) 4:25
2. "No Mercy" (J. Lind, J. Scott) 3:54
3. "The Flame" (B. Mitchell, N. Graham) 5:37
4. "Space" (M. Chapman, H. Knight) 4:16
5. "Never Had a Lot to Lose" (R. Zander, T. Petersson) 3:22
6. "Don't Be Cruel" (O. Blackwell, E. Presley) 3:06
7. "Wrong Side of Love" (R. Nielsen, Todd Cerney) 3:59
8. "All We Need Is a Dream" (R. Nielsen, R. Zander, G. Giuffria) 4:20
9. "Ghost Town" (R. Nielsen, D. Warren) 4:11
10. "All Wound Up" (R. Zander, T. Petersson, J. Allen) 4:45

Japanese version (2009 reissue)

11. "I Want You to Want Me" (studio version) (R. Nielsen)
12. "I Want You to Want Me" (live version at Budokan) (R. Nielsen)

Singles (side A/side B)

- (1988) "The Flame/Through the Night" - #1 US, #77 UK. #2 Aus, #3 BB Mainstream Rock
- (1988) "Don't Be Cruel/I Know What I Want" (live) - #4 US, #77 UK, #8 BB Mainstream Rock, #13 Aus
- (1988) "Ghost Town/Wrong Side of Love" - #33 US
- (1989) "Never Had a Lot to Lose/Let Go" - #75 US
- (1989) "All We Need Is a Dream/No Mercy"

B-sides and outtakes

- "Through the Night" (R. Nielsen, R. Zander, T, Petersson) - 4:19 (*available on the Sex, America, Cheap Trick box set*)
- "You Want It" (R. Nielsen, R. Zander) - 3:41 (*available on the Sex, America, Cheap Trick box set, and the soundtrack to Say Anything...*)
- "Magical Mystery Tour" (J. Lennon, P. McCartney) - 4:10 (*available on The Greatest Hits*)
- "Money (That's What I Want)" (J. Bradford, B. Gordy, Jr.) - 3:15 (*available on the out of print Caddyshack II soundtrack*)

Production

- Produced by Richie Zito
- Engineered and mixed by Phil Kaffel
- Second engineers: Jim Champagne, Bernard Frings, Mike Tacci, Bob Vogt, Toby Wright

Personnel

- Robin Zander: lead vocals, rhythm guitar
- Rick Nielsen: lead guitar, backing vocals
- Tom Petersson: bass, backing vocals
- Bun E. Carlos: drums, percussion

Source (edited): "http://en.wikipedia.org/wiki/Lap_of_Luxury"

Next Position Please

Next Position Please is a studio album by Cheap Trick, produced by Todd Rundgren and released in 1983. It was the band's seventh studio album and eighth release overall.

Background

Cheap Trick's eighth album *Next Position Please*, is a return to the pop-oriented sound of *In Color*. It was produced by Todd Rundgren. The LP peaked at #61 on the Billboard 200 LP charts.

The album received favorable reviews upon release, and yielded the minor hit singles "I Can't Take It" (as credited, the only Cheap Trick song written solely by lead singer Robin Zander, though actually co-written allegedly with Pete Comita) and the Rick Nielsen-penned "Borderline", which was debuted on The Alan Thicke show. The then-band members (Jon Brant, Bun E. Carlos, Rick Nielsen and Robin Zander) consider it one of their best albums. "I Can't Take It" has become a concert staple over the years. Several of the album's tracks were re-worked older material, such as the title track and "You Talk Too Much."

Physical copies of the album were out of print for several years (with the exception of Japan), but as of April 6, 2010 it has been reissued along with the previous album, *One On One*, on one CD.

Cover art

The album cover is a parody of Bruce Springsteen's pose on the cover of *Born to Run*, with the title making a humorous correlation.

Releases

The original vinyl record included 12 tracks. "You Talk Too Much" and "Don't Make Our Love a Crime" appeared as bonus tracks on the cassette version and later on the CD. The record was originally supposed to include both of these tracks along with two others called "Twisted Heart" and "Don't Hit Me With Love," but Cheap Trick's label at the time, Epic Records, forced the band to include a cover of The Motors' "Dancing the Night Away" and the outtake "You Say Jump" in their place. Rundgren refused to produce "Dancing the Night Away," so the track ended up being produced by the band with Ian Taylor, who had engineered the band's previous album, *One on One*. "Twisted Heart" eventually surfaced on the box set *Sex, America, Cheap Trick*. There was one video shot for this LP; "I Can't Take It."

In 2006, Cheap Trick and Epic/Legacy reissued *Next Position Please* as a digital download, calling it *Next Position Please (The Authorized Version)*. The title refers to the fact that the 13 tracks intended for the original album were restored and sequenced according to the band's wishes, while "You Say Jump" and "Dancing the Night Away" were put at the end as "bonus tracks" along with the previously unreleased track "Don't Hit Me With Love." The track "I Don't Love Here Anymore" is incorrectly titled "I Don't Love Her Anymore."

Track listing

Original version

1. "I Can't Take It" (Zander) – 3:28
2. "Borderline" (Nielsen) – 3:34
3. "I Don't Love Here Anymore" (Nielsen) – 3:51
4. "Next Position Please" (Nielsen) – 2:51
5. "Younger Girls" (Nielsen/Zander) – 3:14
6. "Dancing the Night Away" (Garvey/McMaster) – 4:58
7. "You Talk Too Much" (Nielsen) – 1:55 (Bonus track - Cassette/CD only)
8. "3-D" (Nielsen) – 3:37
9. "You Say Jump" (Nielsen) – 3:06
10. "Y.O.Y.O.Y." (Nielsen) – 4:54
11. "Won't Take No for an Answer" (Nielsen) – 3:13
12. "Heaven's Falling" (Rundgren) – 3:48
13. "Invaders of the Heart" (Nielsen) – 4:00
14. "Don't Make Our Love a Crime" (Nielsen) – 3:43 (Bonus track - Cassette/CD only)

2006 "Authorized" reissue

1. "I Can't Take It"
2. "Borderline"
3. "I Don't Love Here Anymore"
4. "Next Position Please"
5. "Younger Girls"
6. "Don't Make Our Love a Crime"
7. "3-D"
8. "You Talk Too Much"
9. "Y.O.Y.O.Y."
10. "Won't Take No for an Answer"
11. "Heaven's Falling"
12. "Invaders of the Heart"
13. "Twisted Heart"
14. "Don't Hit Me With Love"
15. "You Say Jump"
16. "Dancing the Night Away"

Singles

- 1983 "Dancing the Night Away/Don't Make Our Love A Crime"
- 1983 "Dancing the Night Away/I Want You To Want Me & Ain't That A Shame"
- 1983 "I Can't Take It/You Talk Too Much"
- 1983 "Next Position Please" (Europe)

Outtakes

- "Yardbirds Medley" (Instrumental medley of Yardbirds covers, available on *Bun E.'s Basement Bootlegs "Covers"*)
- "Play By The Rules" (Alternate, instrumental version of "I Don't Love Here Anymore," released on a *Trickfest II* prize cassette)
- "Invaders of the Heart (Unedited Instrumental)" (Also released on the *Trickfest II* prize cassette)

Personnel

Cheap Trick

- Robin Zander – lead vocals, rhythm guitar, keyboards
- Rick Nielsen – lead guitar, backing vocals
- Jon Brant – bass, backing vocals
- Bun E. Carlos – drums, percussion

Additional personnel

- Todd Rundgren – guitar, producer, engineer
- Ian Taylor – producer
- Paul Klingberg – engineer

Source (edited): "http://en.wikipedia.org/wiki/Next_Position_Please"

One on One (Cheap Trick album)

One on One is Cheap Trick's sixth studio album, and seventh release in general. Produced by Roy Thomas Baker, it was released in 1982 via Epic Records and was the first Cheap Trick album to feature new bassist Jon Brant.

Background

Nearly two years after their last LP *All Shook Up*, Cheap Trick released an album full of brash, simple rockers. After original bassist Tom Petersson left the group in 1980, he was replaced by Pete Comita. Comita left the group in the early recording stages of *One On One* and was replaced by Jon Brant. Though this was the first album to feature Brant, most of it was recorded without him. Guitarist Rick Nielsen played bass on all but three tracks ("Saturday At Midnight", "If You Want My Love" and "She's Tight"). Brant's face is partially obscured on the front cover. The song

If You Want My Love is one of Rick's favorite songs he has recorded with the group.

Physical copies of the album were out of print for several years (with the exception of Japan), but as of April 6, 2010 it has been reissued along with the following album Next Position Please on one CD.

Track listing

All tracks written by Rick Nielsen, unless otherwise noted.

1. "I Want You" – 3:02
2. "One on One" – 3:05
3. "If You Want My Love" – 3:36
4. "Oo La La La" (Nielsen, Robin Zander) – 3:14
5. "Lookin' Out For Number One" – 3:44
6. "She's Tight" – 2:58
7. "Time is Runnin'" – 2:19
8. "Saturday at Midnight" (Nielsen, Zander) – 2:58
9. "Love's Got a Hold on Me" (Bun E. Carlos, Nielsen, Zander) – 2:35
10. "I Want Be Man" – 3:19
11. "Four Letter Word" (Nielsen, Zander) – 3:37

Remastered versions include an extended version if If You Want My Love as a bonus track.

Singles

The album yielded three singles: "If You Want My Love", "She's Tight" and "Saturday At Midnight." There were promotional videos made for "She's Tight" and "If You Want My Love." Both received heavy rotation on MTV.

- 1982 "If You Want My Love"/"Four Letter Word" - #45 US Pop, #11 US Rock, #55 UK, #1 Australia
- 1982 "She's Tight"/"All I Really Want" - #65 US Pop
- 1982 "Saturday At Midnight"/"Love's Got A Hold On Me"
- 1982 "I Want You"/"Lookin' Out For Number One" (Europe)

Outtakes and Demos

- "All I Really Want" – 2:32 (B-Side to the "She's Tight" single, also available on the *Sex, America, Cheap Trick* box set)
- "Don't Make Our Love A Crime (Demo)" – 3:34 (Available on the *Sex, America, Cheap Trick* box set)
- "Whatcha Gonna Do About It (Demo)" (Small Faces cover) – 2:38 (Available on the *Bun E.'s Basement Bootlegs* "Covers" album)
- "If You Want My Love (Demo)" – 4:34 (Available on the "Oh Boy (Demo)"/"If You Want My Love (Demo)" promotional single)

Personnel

Cheap Trick

- Robin Zander – lead vocals, rhythm guitar, keyboards
- Rick Nielsen – lead guitar, backing vocals
- Jon Brant – bass, backing vocals
- Bun E. Carlos – drums, percussion

Additional personnel

- Roy Thomas Baker – producer
- Ian Taylor – engineer
- Paul Klingberg – assistant
- George Marino – mastering
- David Michael Kennedy – photographer album cover

Source (edited): "http://en.wikipedia.org/wiki/One_on_One_(Cheap_Trick_album)"

Rockford (album)

Rockford is an album by Cheap Trick, released on June 6, 2006. The album's title refers to Rockford, Illinois, the band's hometown. There was one animated video shot for the song "Welcome to the World." The album was praised by both fans and critics, considering it a return to form for Cheap Trick. Rolling Stone magazine even declared Rockford one of the best rock albums of 2006.

The album cover was used for Rockford's vehicle registration stickers in 2007.

Singles

- (2006) "Perfect Stranger
- (2006) "If It Takes A Lifetime"
- (2006) "Come On, Come On, Come On" (US).

Outtakes

- "Mando Ragga" (Vocal Version)
- "What's In It For You" (Re-worked and re-recorded as "Alive" for the following album "The Latest")
- "Every Single Girl" (Instrumental)

These tracks were released on a promotional-only sampler titled *Works In Progress* in 2005, and the disc also contained alternate/unfinished versions of various album tracks from Rockford.

Source (edited): "http://en.wikipedia.org/wiki/Rockford_(album)"

Special One

Special One is an album by the band Cheap Trick. It was released in 2003 to mixed reviews and features the single "Scent of a Woman." It charted for one week, reaching 128 on the album charts.

Track listing

1. "Scent of a Woman" (R. Nielsen/R. Zander/B.E. Carlos) – 4:48
2. "Too Much" (R. Nielsen/R. Zander/T. Petersson) – 4:42
3. "Special One" (R. Nielsen/R. Zander/T. Petersson/B.E.Carlos/J. Brant) – 4:16
4. "Pop Drone" (R. Nielsen/R. Zander/T. Petersson) – 4:43
5. "My Obsession" (R. Nielsen/R. Zander/T. Petersson/J. Raymond) – 3:34
6. "Words" (R. Nielsen/R. Zander/

T. Petersson) – 4:53
7. "Sorry Boy" (R. Nielsen/R. Zander/T. Petersson/B. Carlos/S. Albini) – 4:25
8. "Best Friend" (R. Nielsen/R. Zander/T. Petersson) – 4:16
9. "If I Could" (R. Nielsen/R. Zander/T. Petersson) – 3:51
10. "Low Life in High Heels" (R. Nielsen/R. Zander/T. Petersson) – 2:49
11. "Hummer" (R. Nielsen/R. Zander/T. Petersson) – 4:17

Japanese version
12. "Special One" (Japanese version)
This version of the song is sung partially in Japanese.

Singles
- (2003) "Scent of a Woman"
- (2003) "My Obsession"
- (2003) "Too Much"

Bonus DVD
A limited edition of the album was available upon release and included five music videos.
1. "Say Goodbye" (from *Cheap Trick* (1997 album))
2. "Hot Love" (from the *Music for Hangovers* DVD)
3. "Hard to Tell" (from the *Silver* DVD)
4. "Woke Up With a Monster" (from *Woke Up With a Monster*)
5. "He's a Whore" (from *Cheap Trick*(1977 album))

Personnel
- Robin Zander: lead vocals, rhythm guitar
- Rick Nielsen: lead guitar, backing vocals
- Tom Petersson: bass, backing vocals
- Bun E. Carlos: drums

Source (edited): "http://en.wikipedia.org/wiki/Special_One"

Standing on the Edge (Cheap Trick album)

Standing on the Edge is an album by the American rock group Cheap Trick, released in 1985. Jack Douglas, the producer of Cheap Trick's debut album *Cheap Trick*, made a return for this release.

Overview

Cheap Trick's LP Standing on the Edge, which peaked at number #35 on Billboard's Hot 100 LP chart in 1985, saw the band return to their standard hard-rocking sound with this album. The album was produced by Jack Douglas, who produced the band's eponymous debut album as well as the Found All The Parts EP. The original plans for the album called for band to return to the rough sound of their first album. However, Douglas backed out of mixing process due to legal issues he was having with Yoko Ono. Mixer Tony Platt was called in, and as a result, the album's production featured keyboards and electronic drums more prominently than the band and Douglas had intended.

The album's most successful single "Tonight It's You", is the most well-known track from the album and also appears on numerous greatest hits compilations. Two promotional music videos were made for the song and both clips received much airplay on MTV.

Track listing
1. "Little Sister" (R. Nielsen) – 3:55
2. "Tonight It's You" (M. Radice/J. Brant/R. Nielsen/R. Zander) – 4:47
3. "She's Got Motion" (R. Nielsen/M. Radice) – 3:17
4. "Love Comes" (R. Zander/R. Nielsen) – 4:40
5. "How About You" (R. Zander/R. Nielsen/M. Radice) – 3:00
6. "Standing on the Edge" (R. Nielsen/R. Zander/M. Radice) – 4:44
7. "This Time Around" (J. Brant/M. Radice/R. Zander/R. Nielsen) – 4:33
8. "Rock All Night" (R. Nielsen/R. Zander/B. Carlos/M. Radice) – 2:51
9. "Cover Girl" (R. Nielsen/M. Radice) – 3:41
10. "Wild Wild Women" (R. Nielsen/R. Zander/B. Carlos/M. Radice) – 4:16

2010 Reissue
11. "Tonight It's You" (Single Version) – 3:31

Singles
- (1985) "Tonight It's You/Wild Wild Women" - #44 US, #8 US Mainstream Rock
- (1985) "Little Sister"
- (1985) "How About You"

Outtakes
- "A Place In France" (Available on the *Sex, America, Cheap Trick* box set)
- "Don't Ever Let Me Go" (Unreleased)
- "Lesson In Love" (Unreleased)
- "X-Rated" (Unreleased)

The unreleased tracks are making their rounds on the bootleg circuit along with several other regular album tracks that are slightly different from the final album versions. These tracks may represent the way the band had intended them to sound.

Background information

Bun E. Carlos insisted on being credited with "acoustic drums" because mixer Tony Platt added the electronic drums that were used on much of the album during post-production.

Song doctor Mark Radice was brought in to help the band with the songwriting process. He played keyboards and co-wrote 8 of the album's 10 tracks. He claims that the majority of "Tonight It's You" was written by himself and Bassist Jon Brant.

Guitarist Rick Nielsen's name is misspelled on the back cover of the original pressing as "Rick Nelson." The Japanese import version has Nielsen's name spelled correctly.

Physical copies of the album were out of print for several years (with the exception of Japan), making the original pressing of the CD somewhat of a collectors' item.

Personnel

- Robin Zander - lead vocals, rhythm guitar
- Rick Nielsen - lead guitar, backing vocals
- Jon Brant - bass, backing vocals
- Bun E. Carlos - drums, percussion

Additional personnel

- Mark Radice - Additional keyboards, vocals
- Jack Douglas - Producer
- Paul Klingberg - Recording engineer, keyboards

Source (edited): "http://en.wikipedia.org/wiki/Standing_on_the_Edge_(Cheap_Trick_album)"

The Doctor (Cheap Trick album)

The Doctor is an album by Cheap Trick, released in 1986. It initially sold 88,000 copies and is widely considered the band's worst album. The album's lone single "It's Only Love" (b/w "Name of the Game"), was released in December 1986 and peaked at number #89 on Billboard's Hot 100 singles chart. The album peaked at #86 in the Billboard 200 LP charts. There was a promotional video made for the single "It's Only Love." The video made history as the first music video to prominently use American Sign Language. This would be the band's last album with bassist Jon Brant.

The original version of "Kiss Me Red" was the theme song to the short-lived TV series, *Dreams*. ELO Part II recorded an orchestrated version of the song as well. "Take Me to the Top" is the only track that has been performed live since promotion for the album ended, and is only performed acoustically. It was played in Cheap Trick's 25th Anniversary concert, and this live version can be found on the *Silver* album.

Physical copies of the album were out of print for several years (with the exception of Japan), making the original pressing of the CD somewhat of a collectors' item.

Track listing

1. "It's Up to You" (R. Nielsen/R. Zander) - 3:50
2. "Rearview Mirror Romance" (R. Nielsen/R. Zander) - 4:33
3. "The Doctor" (R. Nielsen) - 4:03
4. "Are You Lonely Tonight" (R. Zander/R. Nielsen) - 3:47
5. "Name of the Game" (R. Nielsen/R. Zander) - 4:17
6. "Kiss Me Red" (R. Nielsen/B. Steinberg/T. Kelly) - 3:37
7. "Take Me to the Top" (R. Nielsen/R. Zander) - 3:46
8. "Good Girls Go to Heaven (Bad Girls Go Everywhere)" (R. Nielsen/R. Zander) - 3:21
9. "Man-U-Lip-U-Lator" (R. Nielsen/R. Zander/J. Brant) - 3:49
10. "It's Only Love" (R. Nielsen/R. Zander) - 4:45

2010 reissue

11. "It's Only Love" (single version) - 3:30

Singles

- (1986) "It's Only Love/Name of the Game"
- (1986) "Kiss Me Red/Name of the Game" (Europe)

Outtakes and demos

- "Money Is the Route of All Fun" (featuring Roy Wood of The Move, available on the *Sex, America, Cheap Trick* box set)
- "Temptation" (unreleased)
- "Dance to the Drummer" (unreleased)
- "Name of the Game" (alternate version) (appeared on a Trickfest II prize cassette)
- "Fortune Cookie" (demo) (available on the *Sex, America, Cheap Trick* box set)
- "Funk #9" (The Doctor demo) (available on the *Sex, America, Cheap Trick* box set)

"Mighty Wings," the end-cut track to the film "Top Gun" was recorded during the demo sessions.

Source (edited): "http://en.wikipedia.org/wiki/The_Doctor_(Cheap_Trick_album)"

The Latest

The Latest is the sixteenth studio album by the American power pop band Cheap Trick. The album was produced by Cheap Trick, Julian Raymond and Howard Willing and was released on June 23, 2009. The album was issued on standard CD as well as limited pressings of vinyl and 8-Track tapes. The album was released to retailers on July 21, 2009. "The Latest" debuted at number 78 on Billboard's Top 200 Charts.

A video for the cover of Slade's "When The Lights Are Out" has been released. The song was released exclusively through iTunes Australia in November, 2008. The video is also available for viewing via the band's YouTube page. A video was also made for "Sick Man of Europe".

Track listing

1. "Sleep Forever" - 1:37
2. "When The Lights Are Out" (Slade cover) - 3:26
3. "Miss Tomorrow" - 4:11
4. "Sick Man of Europe" - 2:08
5. "These Days" - 2:44

6. "Miracle" - 3:47
7. "Everyday You Make Me Crazy" - 1:17
8. "California Girl" - 2:47
9. "Everybody Knows" - 4:16
10. "Alive" - 3:36
11. "Times of Our Lives" - 3:59
12. "Closer, The Ballad of Burt and Linda" - 3:00
13. "Smile" - 4:12

Trivia

"Sleep Forever" was written in memory of a friend who died.

"Miss Tomorrow" was a B-side from Robin Zander's eponymous 1993 solo album.

"Everyday You Make Me Crazy" was originally written by the band as a Pepsi jingle.

"Alive" is a re-worked version of "What's In It For You", an outtake from the band's previous album *Rockford*.

Personnel

- Robin Zander: lead vocals, rhythm guitar
- Rick Nielsen: lead guitar, background vocals
- Tom Petersson: bass, background vocals
- Bun E. Carlos: drums

Additional musicians

- Julian Raymond: arrangements, additional musician
- Roger Joseph Manning Jr: keyboards
- Bon Harris: programming
- George Doering: acoustic guitar
- Luis Conte: programming
- Bennett Salvay: orchestration
- Jason Falkner: additional musician
- Todd Youth: additional musician

Source (edited): "http://en.wikipedia.org/wiki/The_Latest"

Woke up with a Monster

Woke Up With A Monster is an album by Cheap Trick released on Warner Bros. Records in 1994. It was their first and only album for the label, and peaked at US #123. The boost in sales is often accredited to the group's appearance on the *Late Show with David Letterman* to promote the album. By the time the album came out, there had been a variety of significant changes in the band, both musically and in appearance. The style of music is more on the "grunge" side, due to producer Ted Templeman's much criticized heavy-handed production, and unlike several albums that preceded it, it lacks the electronic instruments. Also, Rick Nielsen grew a once trademark goatee, and Robin Zander's voice also grew noticeably deeper. Shortly after the album's release, Cheap Trick was dropped from the Warner Brothers label. It contains songs co-written with Jim Peterik, Julian Raymond, Todd Cerney, and Mark Spiro. There were two videos shot for this LP; "Woke Up With A Monster" and "You're All I Wanna Do." The band later released a CD only 'cutout' that also featured a live performance of the title track.

The album is now only available as a digital download at various online retailers.

Track listing

1. "My Gang" (T. Petersson, R. Zander, R. Nielsen)
2. "Woke Up With A Monster" (R. Nielsen, T. Petersson, R. Zander)
3. "You're All I Wanna Do" (R. Nielsen, T. Petersson, R. Zander, J. Peterik, J. Raymond, Terry Reid)
4. "Never Run Out Of Love" (R. Nielsen, J. Peterik)
5. "Didn't Know I Had It" (R. Nielsen, Todd Cerney)
6. "Ride The Pony" (R. Zander, Mark Spiro)
7. "Girlfriends" (R. Nielsen, T. Petersson, R. Zander, B. Carlos)
8. "Let Her Go" (Writers/Publishers still pending)
9. "Tell Me Everything" (T. Petersson, R. Nielsen, R. Zander, Michael McDonald, Julian Raymond)
10. "Cry Baby" (T. Petersson, R. Nielsen, R. Zander)
11. "Love Me For A Minute" (R. Zander, R. Nielsen, T. Petersson)

Japanese Version

12. "Sabre Dance"

The band also recorded a cover of John Lennon's "Cold Turkey" during these sessions. It went to the *Working Class Hero: A Tribute to John Lennon* album while an alternate version was released on one of the *Bun E.'s Basement Bootleg* albums.

Singles

- (1994) "Woke Up With A Monster" - #16 US Mainstream Rock
- (1994) "You're All I Wanna Do"/ "Cry Baby"
- (1994) "Girlfriends"
- (1994) "Never Run Out of Love"
- (1994) "Didn't Know I Had It"

Unreleased Outtakes

- "Don't Blame It On Love"
- "All Those Years" (Later re-recorded for the 2006 album *Rockford*)
- "Down, Down" (Later re-recorded with different lyrics in 1996 as "Baby Talk" and released on the 7 inch single *Baby Talk/Brontosaurus*)

Source (edited): "http://en.wikipedia.org/wiki/Woke_up_with_a_Monster"

Bun E. Carlos

Bun E. Carlos, born Brad Carlson, June 12, 1951, is the primary drummer for American rock band Cheap Trick.

He is the band's chief setlister and archivist, and maintains recordings of all the band's shows, some of which have been released under the name 'Bun E's Bootlegs'.

Carlos is left-handed, but has alternated between left and right-handed playing throughout his career. He has few writing credits, the most notable of which is the drum solo track "Who D'King", from the album *All Shook Up* and *Bun E. in a Box* (2004), a drum sample CD.

In the late 1990s Carlos introduced his own line of coffee. At one point he offered a Special Limited Edition hand-signed numbered bag of coffee. He continues to market the brand today.

It was announced in early 2009 that Bun E. Carlos had, together with Hanson singer Taylor Hanson, former Smashing Pumpkins guitarist James Iha and Fountains of Wayne bassist Adam Schlesinger, formed a new band called Tinted Windows. This new project ran alongside each of the artists' main bands. The band played its first publicized gig at SXSW in Austin, Texas on March 20, 2009. Their first album was released on April 21, 2009.

On March 19, 2010, Cheap Trick issued a statement that Carlos is not the current touring drummer for Cheap Trick but that he still remains a band member. Cheap Trick guitarist Rick Nielsen's son Daxx was named in the statement as the touring drummer. Carlos had previously suffered from back problems, the recovery and treatment of which had caused him to miss portions of some Cheap Trick tours.

Equipment

Carlos uses Ludwig Drums, Zildjian cymbals, Remo & Ludwig drumheads, Ludwig & DW hardware, Pro-Mark signature drumsticks, and Wilson gloves.

Ludwig Maple Classic Drums: 6.5" X 14" matching maple Snare (or a 5"X14" Black Beauty Snare) 9" X 13" Rack Tom 16" X 16" Floor Tom 16" X 26" Bass Drum

Zildjian Cymbals: 14" A New Beat Hi-Hats 20" A Medium-Thin Crash 20" K Medium Dry Ride 18" A Medium-Thin Crash

Source (edited): "http://en.wikipedia.org/wiki/Bun_E._Carlos"

Jon Brant

Jon Brant (born February 22, 1955 in Chicago) was the bass player for the band Cheap Trick from 1981 to 1987. In addition to his work with that band, Brant has also played with artists including Chris Spedding, Micki Free, Robert Gordon, Lou Reed, and Diana Ross. He was also bassist for the band Red Siren, or Siren after they legally had to change their name.

When Tom Petersson, the original bassist for Cheap Trick, left in 1980, the three remaining band members chose a much-publicized replacement with Pete Comita. Comita had quit before the end of the year after having only played on Cheap Trick's contributions to the *Heavy Metal* soundtrack. With a new album due out in 1981, Cheap Trick went into the studio, and Rick Nielsen played all the bass and guitar parts himself, while auditioning replacement musicians for the tour. They chose Los Angeles-based, Chicago-born bassist Brant as bassist, who joined and is credited with playing bass on their 1982 album *One on One*, on which he overdubbed the bass parts on three songs for which Nielsen had originally played bass.

Brant played on all of the tracks of the band's next three studio albums and co-wrote the hit "Tonight It's You" from 1985's *Standing on the Edge*. In 1987, when Petersson decided to rejoin the band, he displaced Brant. He remains good friends with drummer Bun E. Carlos to this day, and the two of them occasionally play together in "The Bun E. Carlos Experience", a side-project blues band.

Brant rejoined Cheap Trick briefly on stage to play bass during "If You Want My Love" and "She's Tight" during the band's 25th anniversary concert. In 2004, when Petersson was unable to tour briefly after the birth of his child, Brant re-joined the band for a month of shows as opening act for Aerosmith. Brant started the tour with Cheap Trick a few days after returning from a month long tour of bases in the Middle East. He performed in Baghdad, Djibouti, Africa and the UAE. Brant returned once again in 2007 to Cheap Trick for one show in Augusta, Georgia.

Brant performed with legendary blues artist Lynne Jordan for several years in Chicago, then played for a few years with new age artist Nicholas Gunn. Brant also competes in the equestrian sport of eventing.

Brant performs with Native American artist Micki Free. The two perform regularly at the Hard Rock Hotel and Casino in Florida and other venues around the world.

Source (edited): "http://en.wikipedia.org/wiki/Jon_Brant"

Randy Hogan

Randy "Xeno" Hogan was the original lead singer for the rock band Cheap Trick. He left the band shortly after its formation to join "Straight Up" and was replaced by Robin Zander. Randy went on to become a member of Milwaukee based AOR rock band Crossfire (since renamed Bad Boy), of which he is still a member. The band was inducted into the Wisconsin Area Music Industry's Hall of Fame in 1994. Hogan also has been with the Sleighriders, No Strings Attached, and Three's a Crowd. He also performs numerous events with multi-instrumentalist Mitch Cooper and drummer Brian Bruendl.

Source (edited): "http://en.wikipedia.org/wiki/Randy_Hogan"

Rick Nielsen

Rick Nielsen is the lead guitarist, backing vocalist, and primary songwriter of the rock band Cheap Trick. For the band's first few albums, Nielsen wrote the majority of the material himself. He is well known for having many custom-made guitars from Hamer Guitars, including his famous five-neck guitar.

Career

Nielsen formed Cheap Trick in 1972 with bassist Tom Petersson, another Rockford, Illinois native. Before Cheap Trick, he was in a number of bands, including Grim Reapers and Fuse. The latter recorded a one-off debut album released on Epic Records which sold poorly. After the record failed to gain any attention, the band moved to Philadelphia and the band changed their name to Sick Man Of Europe.

The group toured Europe unsuccessfully in 1972 and returned to Illinois in 1973. Upon their return to Rockford, Nielsen and Petersson renamed the band Cheap Trick after adding drummer Bun E. Carlos and vocalist Randy "Xeno" Hogan. In 1974, Hogan left the band and lead singer Robin Zander joined after his contract with a Wisconsin resort was completed.

Appearance

The look or appearance of Rick Nielsen on stage and in public venues can be traced to several elements. One source is certainly Huntz Hall, of The Bowery Boys fame; Nielsen wears a flipped up old style ball cap, Nielsen's face resembles Huntz Hall, and some of Nielsen's on-stage antics have been compared to Hall as well.

Nielsen's use of the black and white checkerboard motif on his clothing was in line with (if not inspiring) the use in other parts of pop culture. Checkerboard Vans sneakers, made famous in the 1982 movie Fast Times at Ridgemont High, is an example of such use after Nielsen.

Source (edited): "http://en.wikipedia.org/wiki/Rick_Nielsen"

Robin Zander

Robin Zander (born 23 January 1953) is the lead singer and rhythm guitarist for the rock band Cheap Trick.

Early life

Zander was born in Beloit, Wisconsin, the fourth of five children; he has two older brothers, and older and younger sisters.

Zander reportedly was reading books by age three, and learned to play the guitar by age 12. He played with his first group, The Destinations, while in seventh grade. The next year he was with a group called Butterscotch Sundays, playing summer festivals, and after that formed a band called Robin and the Hoods. In high school, Zander sang for three years in the Madrigals, the most demanding of the three choral groups at his school, played basketball and football, and had a part-time job at a sandwich shop.

Cheap Trick

In 1972, Zander was offered the lead singer role in a new band called Cheap Trick by the group's drummer, Bun E. Carlos. At the time, Zander was under contract with a resort in Wisconsin Dells, where he sang and played cover songs, and Cheap Trick had a lead vocalist, Randy "Xeno" Hogan. Hogan left the band around the same time Zander's resort contract expired, and Zander joined Cheap Trick as lead singer. Guitarist Rick Nielsen introduces Zander at concerts as his "favorite lead singer in the whole wide world".

In 1993, Zander released a self-titled solo album.

Zander and his Cheap Trick band mates had cameo roles in the 2003 Eddie Murphy comedy *Daddy Day Care*. Zander continues to perform with Cheap Trick around the world. In 2008, the group played in Japan for the 30th anniversary of their original Budokan album release.

Influence

Zander's vocal style has influenced many other rock singers from 1980s hard rockers such as Joe Elliott of Def Leppard, Vince Neil of Mötley Crüe, Axl Rose of Guns N' Roses, Bret Michaels of Poison, and Sebastian Bach of Skid Row, 1990's punk revivalists, Billy Joe Armstrong of Green Day, to alternative icons Eddie Vedder of Pearl Jam, Kurt Cobain of Nirvana, and Scott Weiland of Stone Temple Pilots.

Personal life

Robin Zander performing in Minneapolis, Minnesota in 2008

Zander currently resides in Safety Harbor, Florida with his wife, Pamela and two children: a son, Robin Zander Jr., and a daughter, Robin-Sailor Zander. He has a Bichon Frise named Daisy Mae that lives with him in Safety Harbor, Florida. He has two children from a previous marriage, Ian and Holland, who currently reside in Rockford, Illinois.

Discography
- *Robin Zander* (1993)

Singles
- "I've Always Got You" (1993), #13 Billboard's Mainstream Rock, from album *Robin Zander*
- "Surrender To Me" with Ann Wilson (1988), from the soundtrack to *Tequila Sunrise*
- "In This Country" (1987), from the soundtrack to *Over the Top*
- "You Send the Rain Away" (1987) duet with Rebbie Jackson, #50 Billboard's R&B Chart

Source (edited): "http://en.wikipedia.org/wiki/Robin_Zander"

Tom Petersson

Tom Petersson (b 9 May 1950) is an American musician, best known as the bassist and sometime guitarist for the rock band Cheap Trick.

Career

Petersson contributes to the writing of music and was the first bassist to play a 12 string bass guitar. Jol Dantzig of Hamer Guitars was the builder of the first 12-string bass, who expanded the 8-string bass concept by building an instrument with four courses of three strings each. The root tuning of each course corresponds to that of a four-string bass and adds two strings tuned in unison one octave above the root string. Originally Hamer built him a 10-string bass, then the 12-string he originally wanted. His 12-string bass debuts on the song "Heaven Tonight".

Petersson plays bass as a second lead guitar on "He's a Whore" from Cheap Trick's debut album. He sings lead vocals on "I Know What I Want", on one of the versions of "Voices" and on live versions of "Waitin' for the Man".

Petersson left Cheap Trick, shortly after the recording of *All Shook Up*, on August 26, 1980. Petersson, however, released the solo album *Tom Petersson and Another Language* and toured the North American club scene with his new group with his then-wife Dagmar. He moved to New York and played shows with his band called Sick Man of Europe, which was the name of a pre-Cheap Trick band he was in with Rick Nielsen.

Petersson rejoined Cheap Trick in 1988 for their *Lap of Luxury* album. Despite going platinum and including the #1 hit song "The Flame", Petersson blamed *Lap of Luxury* for pigeonholing them into a sound that they were not comfortable with, which led to *Busted* and the end of their relationship with Epic.

Petersson continues to record and tour with Cheap Trick. Now on a new label, Cheap Trick Unlimited, Cheap Trick released *Rockford* in June 2006 and *The Latest* in June 2009. Petersson also appeared on Frank Black's *Fast Man Raider Man* album, released in June 2006.

Personal life

Petersson is married to wife Alison Petersson. He has a son, Liam, and a daughter, Lila.

Other work

Petersson was in Concrete Blonde's video for their song "Someday?".

Source (edited): "http://en.wikipedia.org/wiki/Tom_Petersson"

Ain't That a Shame

"**Ain't That a Shame**" is a song by Fats Domino and Dave Bartholomew, recorded in New Orleans, Louisiana, for Imperial Records and released in 1955. The original recording ("**Ain't It a Shame**") was a hit for Domino, eventually selling a million copies. It reached #1 on the "Black Singles" chart and #10 on the "Pop Singles" chart. The song is ranked #431 on the *Rolling Stone* magazine's list of The 500 Greatest Songs of All Time.

The song gained national fame after being re-recorded by white recording artist Pat Boone. Domino's version soon became more popular, bringing Domino's music to the mass market a half dozen years after his first major recording, "The Fat Man".

After "Ain't It a Shame", mainstream artists began covering Domino's songs. Teresa Brewer, for instance, performed the Domino rewrite of a folk song called "Bo Weevil".

According to legend, Pat Boone suggested the title and lyrics be altered to "Isn't That A Shame" to make it more appealing to a broader audience but was dissuaded by his producers. Despite his suggestion being rejected, Boone had his first *Billboard* number-one single in 1955. Domino complimented Boone's cover of the song. Boone likes to tell the story about a Fats Domino concert and Domino invited Boone on stage. Domino showed a big gold ring and said "Pat Boone bought me this ring."

This was the first song that John Lennon learned to play. He later covered it on *Rock 'n' Roll*.

On the screen

Fats Domino can be seen performing this song in a 1956 film *Shake, Rattle & Rock!*. The song is heard in *American Graffiti*, and is used in the movies *October Sky*, *L.A. Story*, *School Ties* and *Mischief*. As of April 2007 the song can be heard in commercials for Dr Pepper. It can be heard at the end of the Season Four finale of the television series The

Shield. It was also included in the soundtrack for the 2010 video game Mafia II.

Covers

- Pat Torpey in 1999 on Y2K.
- Paul McCartney in 1990 on *Tripping the Live Fantastic*. Recorded live during his Japanese tour.
- Cheap Trick in 1979. It charted at #35 after being released on their live album *At Budokan*. (Reportedly Fats Domino's favorite cover)
- Brownsville Station in 1977 on Brownsville Station album.
- Tanya Tucker in 1976 on Lovin' and Learnin'.
- John Lennon in 1975 on *Rock 'n' Roll*. Lennon's version is also the opening track on the 2007 tribute album *Goin' Home: A Tribute to Fats Domino* (Vanguard Records).
- Gary Glitter in 1972 on the LP Glitter.
- The Four Seasons in 1963 on Ain't That A Shame and 11 Others
- Pat Boone in 1955. It hit #1 for two weeks on the *Billboard Most Played in Jukeboxes* charts.
- Sea Monk Seven in 2006

Source (edited): "http://en.wikipedia.org/wiki/Ain%27t_That_a_Shame"

California Man (song)

California Man is a song by The Move.

Released in 1972 as a maxi single with "Do Ya" and "Ella James" as a double B-side, this was The Move's last official single release. The Electric Light Orchestra, originally conceived as a side-project to The Move, issued its first single,10538 Overture, a month after this track. A pastiche of Jerry Lee Lewis, Little Richard and Larry Williams, the composition is recorded in a high energy rock 'n' roll style, with lead vocals by both Jeff Lynne and Roy Wood, then jointly leaders of both ELO and The Move. California Man reached No. 7 on the UK Singles Chart in May 1972.

In the U.S. the single was issued on the United Artists record label. It was flipped after release, when Lynne's "Do Ya" b-side proved more popular. It became The Move's only US charting single, peaking at 93 on the Billboard Hot 100 in November 1972.

Only Wood, Lynne and drummer Bev Bevan appear on the recording. The picture sleeve opposite has an older picture of The Move, including bassist Rick Price, who was no longer a member of the group by then.

The Move's version of the song never originally appeared on one of their studio albums, however it does appear as a bonus track on the reissue of Message From the Country.

The song was later covered by Cheap Trick and Jim Davidson. Cheap Trick included it on their 1978 album *Heaven Tonight* and also released it as a single that year as a follow up to "Surrender". It has also been included on several Cheap Trick compilation albums. Cliff Richard has performed it live on occasion.

Ella James

Ella James was a song taken from the band's final album Message From the Country. written by Roy Wood.

It was released as a single in the UK in 1971 with **No Time** from the same album on the flip side, but was quickly withdrawn in favour of **Tonight**, and later ended up being a double B-side of **California Man** along with Do Ya on the aforementioned single.

The song was covered by The Nashville Teens.

Source (edited): "http://en.wikipedia.org/wiki/California_Man_(song)"

Clock Strikes Ten

"**Clock Strikes Ten**" is a song released in 1977 by Cheap Trick on their second album, *In Color*. It was written by Cheap Trick guitarist Rick Nielsen. It was released as a single in Japan, where it was a major hit and reached #1 on their singles chart. Its success, as well as the success of two follow up singles, "I Want You to Want Me" and "Surrender", paved the way for Cheap Trick's famous concerts at Nippon Budokan in Tokyo in April 1978 that were recorded for the group's most popular album *Cheap Trick at Budokan*.

Content

It is a fast paced song that begins with guitar notes struck to sound like chimes (Westminster chimes, full hour). The song has similarities to the 1950s song "Rock Around the Clock". Nielsen has described the theme of the song as "Simple fun and games. People are going out on a Saturday night, going completely nuts, people that live for the weekend, and who doesn't?"

In popular culture

"Clock Strikes Ten" was often played as an encore in live shows, and it was the final song played in the encore of the Budokan concerts. The live version was released as the final song on the *Cheap Trick at Budokan* album. The live version was also released as the B-side of the live version single of "I Want You to Want Me" that was a top 10 hit in 1979. In 1978, Cheap Trick played "Clock Strikes Ten" and "I Want You to Want Me" on the BBC2 television program *The Old Grey Whistle Test*. "Clock Strikes Ten" has since been released on several other compilation and live albums, including *The Greatest Hits, Sex, America, Cheap Trick, The Essential Cheap Trick* and *Live in Australia*. It has also been covered by The Electric

Day Tripper

"**Day Tripper**" is a song by The Beatles, released as a double A-side single with "We Can Work It Out". Both songs were recorded during the sessions for the *Rubber Soul* album. The single topped the UK Singles Chart and the song peaked at number five on the *Billboard* Hot 100 chart in January, 1966.

Composition

Main Guitar Riff

Under the pressure of needing a new single for the Christmas market, John Lennon wrote the music, including the famous guitar hook, and most of the lyrics, while Paul McCartney helped with the verses.

"Day Tripper" was a typical play on words by Lennon: "Day trippers are people who go on a day trip, right? Usually on a ferryboat or something. But [the song] was kind of . . . you're just a weekend hippie. Get it?" In the same interview Lennon said, "That's mine. Including the lick, the guitar break and the whole bit." In his 1970 interview with *Rolling Stone*, however, he used "Day Tripper" as one example of their collaboration, where one partner had the main idea but the other took up the cause and completed it. For his part, McCartney claimed it was very much a collaboration based on Lennon's original idea.

In *Many Years From Now*, McCartney said that "Day Tripper" was about drugs, and "a tongue-in-cheek song about someone who was ... committed only in part to the idea." The line recorded as "she's a big teaser" was originally written as "she's a prick teaser."

According to music critic Ian MacDonald, the song "starts as a twelve-bar blues in E, which makes a feint at turning into a twelve-bar in the relative minor (i.e. the chorus) before doubling back to the expected B—another joke from a group which had clearly decided that wit was to be their new gimmick." Indeed, in 1966 McCartney said in *Melody Maker* that "Day Tripper" and "Drive My Car" (recorded three days prior) were "funny songs, songs with jokes in." McCartney provides the lead vocal for the verses and Lennon the harmony, in contrast to the Beatles' usual practice of a song's principal composer singing lead, although Lennon sings lead in the chorus, with McCartney on harmony.

Recording

The song was recorded on 16 October 1965. The Beatles recorded the basic rhythm track for "If I Needed Someone" after completing "Day Tripper".

The released master contains one of the most noticeable mistakes of any Beatles song, a drop out at 1:50 in which the lead guitar and tambourine momentarily disappears, or drops out. There are also two more minor drop outs at 1:56 and 2:32. Bootleg releases of an early mix (which present an extended breakdown as opposed to a polished fadeout) feature a technical glitch on the session tape itself, with characteristics of an accidental recording over the original take as the recorder comes up to speed. This was later fixed on the 2000 compilation *1* and on the remastered *Past Masters*. Though not released on any album in the United Kingdom (until *A Collection of Beatles Oldies*, in 1966, and later on *1962–1966*, aka the *Red Album*, released in 1973), it was released in the US on the album *Yesterday and Today*.

Music video

The Beatles filmed three different music videos, directed by Joe McGrath.

Personnel

- John Lennon – lead vocal (chorus), harmony vocal (verses), rhythm guitar, lead guitar (solo)
- Paul McCartney – lead vocal (verses), harmony vocal (chorus), bass
- George Harrison – harmony vocal (chorus), lead guitar (riff)
- Ringo Starr – drums, tambourine

Personnel per Ian MacDonald and Mark Lewisohn.

Cover versions

- The Jimi Hendrix Experience covered this song on *BBC Sessions*.
- Mae West covered the song on her 1966 album *Way Out West*. The album was re-released in 2008 on CD.
- Otis Redding's version is available on *Complete & Unbelievable: The Otis Redding Dictionary of Soul*.
- Sergio Mendes & Brasil '66 covered this song on *Herb Alpert Presents*
- Anne Murray covered this song on *Highly Prized Possession*
- Whitesnake covered this song on *Trouble*
- Electric Light Orchestra covered this song on the *Long Beach* live album
- James Taylor covered this song on *Flag*
- Cheap Trick covered this song on the *Found All the Parts* EP
- Sham 69 covered this song on *The Game*
- Yellow Magic Orchestra covered this song on the 1979 album *Solid State Survivor*
- Daniel Ash covered this song on *Coming Down*
- Gene Wooten covered this song on *The Great Dobro Sessions*
- Ocean Colour Scene covered this song with members of Oasis on a single
- Tok tok tok covered this song on *50 Ways To Leave Your Lover*
- Ian Hunter covered this song on *Missing In Action*
- The Punkles covered this song on *Pistol*
- Tommy Shaw covered this song on *Butchering the Beatles: A Headbashing Tribute*
- David Cook covered this song on *Day Tripper (American Idol Studio*

- Bad Brains covered this song in dub reggae format as a staple at live shows during the tour for *I Against I*.
- Type O Negative recorded a medley of Beatles' songs including this one on "World Coming Down"
- Lulu covered this song in 1967 on her album *Love Loves to Love Lulu*
- Nancy Sinatra covered the song on her album *Boots*
- Fever Tree covered the song on their album *Fever Tree* in a medley with "We Can Work It Out".
- Budos Band used the melody in their song *Reppirt Yad* (*Day Tripper* spelled in reverse) on their album *Budos Band III*.
- J. J. Barnes covered this song on a single released on the Ric-Tic label in 1966.
- Ramsey Lewis covered this song on the 1966 album *Wade in the Water (album)*.

The song is playable in the music video game *The Beatles: Rock Band*.

Source (edited): "http://en.wikipedia.org/wiki/Day_Tripper"

Don't Be Cruel

For the Bobby Brown album, see Don't Be Cruel (album).
For the Bobby Brown song, see Don't Be Cruel (Bobby Brown song).

"**Don't Be Cruel**" is a song recorded by Elvis Presley and published by Elvis Presley Music and written by Otis Blackwell in 1956. It was inducted into the Grammy Hall of Fame in 2002. In 2004, it was listed #197 in *Rolling Stone's* list of 500 Greatest Songs of All Time. The song is currently ranked as the 92nd greatest song of all time, as well as the fifth best song of 1956, by Acclaimed Music.

Elvis Presley

Recording

"Don't Be Cruel" was the first song that Presley's song publishers, Hill and Range, brought to him to record. Blackwell was more than happy to give up 50% of the royalties and a co-writing credit to Presley to ensure that the "hottest new singer around covered it".

Presley recorded the song on July 2, 1956 during an exhaustive recording session at RCA studios in New York City. During this session he also recorded "Hound Dog", and "Any Way You Want Me". The song featured Presley's regular band of Scotty Moore on lead guitar (with Presley usually providing rhythm guitar), Bill Black on bass, D. J. Fontana on drums, and backing vocals from the Jordanaires. The producing credit was given to RCA's Steve Sholes, although the studio recordings reveal that Presley produced the songs in this session by selecting the song, reworking the arrangement on piano, and insisting on 28 takes before he was satisfied with it. He also ran through 31 takes of "Hound Dog".

Release

The single was released on July 13, 1956 backed with "Hound Dog". Within a few weeks "Hound Dog" had risen to #2 on the Pop charts with sales of over one million. Soon after it was overtaken by "Don't Be Cruel" which took #1 on all three main charts; Pop, Country, and R 'n' B. Between them, both songs remained at #1 on the Pop chart for a run of 11 weeks tying it with the 1950 Anton Karas hit "The Third Man Theme" and the 1951/1952 Johnnie Ray hit "Cry" for the longest stay at number one by a single record until 1992's smash "End of the Road" by Boyz II Men. By the end of 1956 it had sold in excess of four million copies.

Presley performed "Don't Be Cruel" during all three of his appearances on *The Ed Sullivan Show* in September 1956 and January 1957.

Legacy

"Don't Be Cruel" went on to become Presley's biggest selling single recorded in 1956, with sales over six million by 1961. It became a regular feature of his live sets until his death in 1977, and was often coupled with "Jailhouse Rock" or "Teddy Bear" during performances from 1969.

Many artists including Barbara Lynn (1963, Jamie #1244 45 RPM), Bill Black Combo, Billy Swan, Cheap Trick, The Judds, Merle Haggard, John Lennon, Jerry Lee Lewis, Neil Diamond, Jackie Wilson, and Roland Cedermark have recorded the song. Presley was said to be so impressed with Wilson's version that he would later incorporate many of Wilson's mannerisms into future performances. Debbie Harry recorded the song for the Otis Blackwell tribute album "Brace Yourself! A Tribute to Otis Blackwell". Cheap Trick's version of this song became a hit when it reached #4 on the Billboard Hot 100 in 1988.

The main bass riff of the song is also used as the background music in the Nintendo video game Donkey Kong.

Jonathan Rhys Meyers lip-synched the original version of the song in a scene from *Elvis*, where it shows him performing at the Jacksonville Theatre.

Source (edited): "http://en.wikipedia.org/wiki/Don%27t_Be_Cruel"

Dream Police (song)

"**Dream Police**" is the title of a song written by Rick Nielsen and originally released in 1979 by the American rock band Cheap Trick. It was the title track of Cheap Trick's album *Dream Police*. The single peaked #26 on the US single chart.

Critical reception

Tom Maginnis of Allmusic described the song as "a tongue in cheek Orwellian nightmare."

In popular culture

- The song was covered in 2010 by Rob Gravelle, former guitarist of Ivory Knight, and released as a digital MP3 single.
- The song was featured in the movie *Hard Rock Treasures*.
- The song was featured in the *Simpsons* episode *Two Bad Neighbors* Apu is seen singing the chorus.
- The song is featured as a playable track in the video game *Guitar Hero: Aerosmith*.
- The song was partially sung by the character Mike Damone in the movie *Fast Times at Ridgemont High* to try and drum up a (scalped) ticket sale.
- The song is featured on the Rite Aid Radio network, broadcasted to Rite Aid Pharmacies across the country.
- The song was referenced in the TV series *United States of Tara*. The manager of the restaurant where the protagonist's daughter works, is seen singing it to her(the daughter) before they proceed to make out.
- *Jim Norton* of the *Opie and Anthony Show* has referred to this song as the "Suck Police".
- The song was featured in the *Lost* episode *The Lie*.
- The name of the song was mentioned on the series *Life on Mars*, where the police were telling Sam that they live inside his head.
- In 2010, Cheap Trick re-recorded Dream Police as "Green Police," a spoof of police who arrest people for acts deemed to be damaging to the environment. The song was the focus of a commercial played during Super Bowl XLIV for Audi.
- The song was covered by prominent punk rock band No Use for a Name, which featured on the Fat Wreck Chords compilation Harder, Fatter + Louder!
- The song was used in the promo commercials for the second season of *Superjail!*

Source (edited): "http://en.wikipedia.org/wiki/Dream_Police_(song)"

Elo Kiddies

"ELO Kiddies" is a glam-style song by Cheap Trick, released in 1977 on the album *Cheap Trick*. It was released as a single twice, in 1977 as an A-side backed by "Speak Now Or Forever Hold Your Peace" and in 1979, as the B-side the live "Ain't That a Shame" from *Cheap Trick at Budokan*.

References

Source (edited): "http://en.wikipedia.org/wiki/Elo_Kiddies"

I Want You to Want Me

"**I Want You to Want Me**" is a song by Cheap Trick which first appeared on their second album *In Color* in 1977. It was the first single released from that album but it didn't chart in the US. However, it was a #1 single in Japan. Its success in Japan, as well as the success of its preceding single "Clock Strikes Ten" and its followup "Surrender", paved the way for Cheap Trick's famous concerts at Nippon Budokan in Tokyo in April 1978 that were recorded for the group's most popular album, *Cheap Trick at Budokan*. A live version of "I Want You to Want Me" from the album *Cheap Trick at Budokan* was released in 1979 and became their biggest selling single, reaching #7 on the Billboard Hot 100. It was certified Gold by the Recording Industry Association of America, representing sales of one million records. In Canada, it reached #2 in on the *RPM* national singles chart, remaining there for two weeks. It was also the band's highest charting single in Britain, where it reached #29.

The single was certified Gold in Canada for the sale of 5,000 singles in September 1979.

All appearances

- 1977: *In Color*
- 1978: *From Tokyo to You*
- 1978: *Cheap Trick at Budokan*
- 1991: *The Greatest Hits*
- 1991: *Queens Logic* soundtrack
- 1997: *Private Parts* soundtrack
- 1998: *Cheap Trick (1998 Reissue)*
- 1998: *Cheap Trick at Budokan: The Complete Concert*
- 1999: *That '70s Album (Rockin')*
- 1999: *Music for Hangovers*
- 2000: *Authorized Greatest Hits*

Cover versions

- Tigertailz - *Young and Crazy* (1987) (bonus track on re-release)
- Rob & Fab - *Rob & Fab* (1993) (added two verses of rapping)
- Propagandhi – *How To Clean Everything* (1993)
- Letters to Cleo – *10 Things I Hate About You* soundtrack (1999)
- Dwight Yoakam – *Tomorrow's Sounds Today* (2000)
- SR-71 - *Here We Go Again* (2004)
- Lindsay Lohan – *A Little More Personal (Raw)* (2005)
- Chris Isaak – *Best of Chris Isaak* (2006)
- Gael García Bernal – *Rudo y Cursi* soundtrack, Spanish language cover entitled "*Quiero Que Me Quieras*" (2008)
- Los Odio featuring Juan Son – *Rudo y Cursi* soundtrack (2008)
- Quiero Club – *Rudo y Cursi* soundtrack (2008)
- Damhnait Doyle – *Lights Down Low* (2008)
- KSM - *Read Between the Lines* (2009)

- Aly Michalka – *Bandslam* soundtrack (2009)
- Holmes Brothers - *State Of Grace* (2007)
- XXX (band) - "Heaven, Hell Or Hollywood?" (2009)
- The Knockouts - Diamond Prime Music / Sound Pollution AB(2011)

In popular culture

Before every show Stephen Colbert psychs himself up by playing the *At Budokan* version of this song.
Source (edited): "http://en.wikipedia.org/wiki/I_Want_You_to_Want_Me"

Mighty Wings

"**Mighty Wings**" is a rock song written by Harold Faltermeyer and Mark Spiro, performed by American group Cheap Trick in 1985 (released as a single in 1985). It appeared on the soundtrack for the *Top Gun* film, which was released in May 1986 and lasts 3 minutes 51 seconds.

In the film *Top Gun*, the music (without the lyrics) played in the first training session at Miramar, while the full version with the lyrics played as the credits rolled over the sunset at the end of the film.
Source (edited): "http://en.wikipedia.org/wiki/Mighty_Wings"

Need Your Love (song)

Need Your Love is a song written by Rick Nielsen and Tom Petersson that was originally performed by American rock band Cheap Trick. The song was originally recorded for Cheap Trick's 1979 album *Dream Police*. However, a live version was included on the 1979 live album *Cheap Trick at Budokan*, which ended up being released in the United States before *Dream Police* was released. It was included on *Cheap Trick at Budokan*, which was originally intended for release only in Japan and not in the U.S., because the band's Japanese label demanded that three new songs be included on the live album. It has been covered by several other artists, including Tony Rebel and Shadow Reef.

The song on uses a traditional hard rock formula, and does not use synthesized strings as were used on other songs on *Dream Police*. The musical backing to the song on *Dream Police* is basically a mid-tempo jam consisting of Nielsen's fancy guitar playing and Petersson's driving bass. Singer Robin Zander sings in a falsetto voice and incorporates a tremolo warble at the end of each line. Nielsen has commented that "I think it is a desperate type of tune that Robin does a great job of singing." This arrangement is put through several changes, incorporating a heavy guitar break, which stretches the length of the song more than seven and a half minutes. Ira Robbins of *Trouser Press* notes that the song "starts out slow and restrained, but builds to an intense boogie-based climax." Music critic Dave Marsh of *Rolling Stone Magazine* described the song as "a better version of the Who meets Free than Bad Company has ever managed — but that's about all it is." *Mojo* noted that "Need Your Love" and "Gonna Raise Hell", another song from *Dream Police*, "proved the Trick could do heavy, freaky rock jams as well as any of their peers."

The live version of the song on *Cheap Trick at Budokan* is not very different from the version on *Dream Police*. It begins with Zander proclaiming "I need your love" to the screaming female fans. This is followed by Bun E. Carlos' pounding drumming that leads into Nielsen's and Petersson's guitar and bass work. The song builds to a steady climax and then transforms itself into a supercharged boogie. Carlos has stated that the band originally learned the song for their 1978 album *Heaven Tonight* but it was only when producer Tom Werman heard them play the band live that he realized how good the song was and regretted excluding it from the earlier album.

Subsequent to its initial releases, the song was released on Cheap Trick compilation albums *Hits of Cheap Trick*, *The Music of Cheap Trick* and *Setlist: The Very Best of Cheap Trick Live*.
Source (edited): "http://en.wikipedia.org/wiki/Need_Your_Love_(song)"

Surrender (Cheap Trick song)

"**Surrender**" is a single by Cheap Trick released in June 1978 from the album *Heaven Tonight*. It was the first Cheap Trick single to enter the Billboard Hot 100 chart, peaking at number 62. But it was a hit single in Japan and its success in Japan, as well as the success of its preceding singles "Clock Strikes Ten" and "I Want You to Want Me", paved the way for Cheap Trick's famous concerts at Nippon Budokan in Tokyo in April 1978 that were recorded for the group's most popular album *Cheap Trick at Budokan*. It is ranked #465 on the *Rolling Stone* magazine's list of "the 500 Greatest Songs of All Time".

Content

It is a late 1970s teen anthem, describing the relations between the baby boomer narrator and his G.I. generation parents. The narrator describes how his parents are weirder and hipper than many children would believe. For example, the narrator describes how he discovers his "mom and dad are rolling on the couch" and listening to his Kiss records late at night ("rolling numbers, rock-and-rolling, got my Kiss records out").

Live performances

The counter-choral of "We're all alright!", repeated four times in the final chorus of the song, has become an audience favorite, with the band members often leading the entire audience in numerous, shouted repetitions of the phrase. In a 2008 interview, Rick Nielsen stated: "When I wrote the song, the 'we're all alright' was originally only intended to refer to the four of us; that's why it comes right after the 'Bun-E/Tom/Robin/Rick's alright' section. After we started playing it live however, I came to realize that, to our audience, it was inclusive of all of us - our generation; that we're ALL alright, we survived the 60s & Vietnam & Nixon & everything, and we're all still here, playing music and having fun. That's when we started playing with it a little in concert; I'll tell ya, you get 50 - 60 thousand people screaming 'WE'RE ALL ALRIGHT!' in unison, that's a pretty positive affirmation!" Cheap Trick still performs this song, and Rick Nielsen often throws Kiss records to the audience in live performances at the moment Kiss is mentioned in the song.
Source (edited): "http://en.wikipedia.org/wiki/Surrender_(Cheap_Trick _song)"

The Flame (Cheap Trick song)

"**The Flame**" is a hit power ballad by Cheap Trick, released on July 25, 1988. The song was first offered to English singer Elkie Brooks, who turned it down. Written by Bob Mitchell and Nick Graham, the song was initially released on Cheap Trick's *Lap of Luxury* album. "The Flame" reached number one on the American Billboard Hot 100 in 1988 when issued as a single; it also reached number one in Australia and Canada. The success of the song brought the group out of a years-long commercial slump and back into music industry prominence.

Background

According to lead vocalist Robin Zander, "The band was very skeptical about performing this song live, because we only liked to perform songs written by us. However, a young man from, oh, I don't know, somewhere, confirmed to us after a show in Florida about a week after the song was released that the song was great and, get this, would be a #1 single. As we joked about the guy's prediction, we later realized whoa! This guy was right. I thank him for that."

In Popular Culture

- "The Flame" was covered in 1998 by electronic dance music singer Erin Hamilton. Included on her 1999 album *One World*, the song was a top-twenty hit on the U.S. Hot Dance Club Play chart. Nine years later, the song was remixed and re-released as "The Flame 08" and this version went to number one on the U.S. dance chart, becoming Hamilton's first chart-topper.
- In 2004, "The Flame" was performed on the second season of *Australian Idol* by eventual winner Casey Donovan on the Final 6 80's theme night. Donovan recorded the song as her cover song on the series cast album, *Australian Idol Season 2 The Final 10 Cast Album*.The Flame seemed an odd choice for Donovan's cover on the cast album because even though she was praised for the performance, there were several other performances where she received a "Touchdown" from judge Mark Holden and this wasn't one of them.After this performance, Donovan was placed in the Bottom two for the first time on the verdict show, which further adds to this being an odd choice for this to be her cast album cover.
- This song is also covered by Greg Bowler in his forthcoming (2010) album "Korean Karaoke Knights". It is closely aligned to the artist's established style of challenging established genre norms, being an acid house fusion of Finnish humppa and reggae.
- In *The Looney Tunes Show* episode, "Fish and Visitors", Yosemite Sam briefly sings 'The Flame' on karaoke.

Source (edited): "http://en.wikipedia.org/wiki/The_Flame_(Cheap_Trick _song)"

Voices (Cheap Trick song)

"**Voices**" is the title of a song written by Rick Nielsen and recorded from American rock band Cheap Trick which appeared on the album Dream Police. It was written by guitarist Rick Neilsen. The single was released in 1979 and peaked at #32 in the US. The single has become one of the band's more widely known tracks.

The song was originally recorded with Cheap Trick bass guitar player Tom Petersson singing the lead vocal, but it was later rerecorded for the *Dream Police* album with Cheap Trick's usual lead vocalist, Robin Zander, singing the lead. On the released track, Petersson and Nielsen provide back up vocals. The song is unusual for Cheap Trick in that six or seven vocal tracks are layered in, making it impossible to replicate the sound on the album in live concerts. Steve Lukather of the band Toto plays acoustic guitar on the version of the song on *Dream Police*, but is uncredited.

Prior to its release on *Dream Police*, "Voices", backed by "Surrender", was released as a single in the UK as a promotion for the upcoming album. However, when the album release was delayed, the single was quickly pulled. When *Dream Police* was finally on the verge of being released, Arnold Levine directed a promotional film of the band featuring "Voices" and two other songs from the album, "Dream Police" and "Way of the World".

Subsequent to its original release on *Dream Police*, "Voices" has appeared on several Cheap Trick compilation albums, including *The Greatest Hits*, *The Essential Cheap Trick*, *Collections*, *Playlist: The Very Best of Cheap Trick* and *The Music of Cheap Trick* and the box set *Sex, America, Cheap Trick*. A number of live versions have also been released. A performance from August 28, 1999 at Davis Park in Rockford, Illinois was released on *Silver*. A 2008 performance at Nippon Budokan, Tokyo was released on the DVD in the 30th anniversary edition *Cheap Trick at Budokan*. In 1980, Zander and Nielsen performed the song during an appearance on the television show *Kids Are People Too*.

Critical reception

Critic Rick Clark of Allmusic described "Voices" as being "appealing melodic (albeit wimpy)" and Stephen Thomas Erlewine, also of Allmusic described it as one of Cheap Tricks finest songs. Critic Robert Coyne considers "Voices" to be Nielsen's "best ever ballad," but Dave Marsh of Rolling Stone Magazine described is as "disastrous" and "a ballad from a band that has absolutely no facility for ballads."

Cover versions

Jon Brion covered "Voices" on his 2001 debut album *Meaningless*.

Other media

The song is featured in the How I Met Your Mother episode "The Pineapple Incident" where Ted has a hangover and Ted, Marshall, Lily and Barney have to find out the entire story by telling it from their point of view. The song is played when Ted gets drunk and calls Robin and plays the song on the jukebox and starts singing it until he falls over. Earlier in the episode, the show uses the guitar solo from the song during a sequence when Ted had passed out.

Source (edited): "http://en.wikipedia.org/wiki/Voices_(Cheap_Trick_song)"